Strategies for Integrating Reading and Writing
in Middle and High School Classrooms

Strategies for Integrating Reading and Writing in Middle and High School Classrooms

by
Karen D. Wood
&
Janis M. Harmon

National Middle School Association
Westerville, Ohio

National Middle School Association
4151 Executive Parkway
Suite 300
Westerville, Ohio 43081
Telephone (800) 528-NMSA
www.nmsa.org

Printed in the United States of America.
Fourth Printing, April 2005

Sue Swaim, Executive Director
Jeff Ward, Deputy Executive Director
April Tibbles, Director of Publications
Edward Brazee, Editor, Professional Publications
John Lounsbury, Consulting Editor, Professional Publications
Mary Mitchell, Designer and Editorial Assistant
Sarah Varughese, Cover Design
Marcia Meade-Hurst, Senior Publications Representative

Library of Congress Cataloging-in-Publication Data

Wood, Karen D.
    Strategies for integrating reading and writing in middle and high school classrooms/ by Karen D. Wood, Janis M. Harmon.
        p. cm.
    Includes bibliographical references.
    ISBN 1-56090-172-1 (pbk.)
        1. Language arts (Middle school) 2. Language arts (Secondary) I. Harmon Janis M., date- II. Title

LB1631 .W59 2001
428.1'071'2--dc21   2001045035

... to my husband, David, and my children Eric, Ryan, Lauren, and Kevin
— K.D.W.

... to my husband, Phil, and my sons, Phillip and Joseph
— J. M. H.

Table of Contents

About the Authors

Karen Wood is a Professor in the Department of Reading and Elementary Education at the University of North Carolina at Charlotte where she was the first recipient of the College of Education's Excellence in Teaching Award. A former reading teacher, reading specialist, and K-12 instructional coordinator in the public schools, Dr. Wood's professional emphasis is on translating research and theory into classroom practice including areas such as: flexible grouping, integrating reading/language arts across the curriculum, including diverse learners in the classroom community, and practical strategies for teaching content area literacy.

Dr. Wood originated the "Out of Research – Into Practice" column for the *Middle School Journal* in 1986 and continues as its author today. She has written over 150 articles and chapters and was co-editor of the journal *Reading Research and Instruction*. Her books include: *Guiding Readers Through Text; Exploring Literature in the Classroom; Teaching Reading to High Risk Learners; Promoting Literacy in Grades 4-9: A Handbook for Teachers and Administrators;* and *Literacy Strategies Across the Subject Areas*.

Janis M. Harmon is an associate professor in the College of Education and Human Development at the University of Texas at San Antonio where she received the President's Distinguished Achievement Award for Teaching Excellence in 2001. She has 21 years of experience teaching middle school students in Louisiana and has also served as a reading instructional specialist. She received her Ph.D. in Educational Theory and Practice from The Ohio State University and a M.Ed. and Educational Specialist Degree from the University of Southwestern Louisiana in Lafayette.

Dr. Harmon has published articles in such journals as *Research in the Teaching of English, Journal of Literacy Research, Journal of Adolescent and Adult Literacy, Middle School Journal, Elementary School Journal,* and the *National Reading Conference Yearbook.* Her primary interests are promoting and researching effective middle school literacy programs with a special emphasis on vocabulary acquisition and instruction for middle school learners.

Preface

As a former middle school reading teacher, I recall how my colleagues and I eagerly searched for practical teaching ideas to enliven a vocabulary lesson, help a class comprehend a textbook, or spark interest in the eyes of a student struggling to write a sentence. Later, as a K-12 reading coordinator, I realized how great this need is at the high school level as well. Teachers of content at the middle and high school levels are specialists in their respective fields. Most have had only one content area literacy course at the college level, often long before they understood how important the concept was and how many more questions and concerns they would have as they proceeded in their careers.

While the thinking behind this new book is rooted in my days as a classroom teacher and reading coordinator, its true origin began in 1986 when John Lounsbury, then editor of the *Middle School Journal* and now a publications editor for the National Middle School Association, gave the stamp of approval to initiate the "Out of Research: Into Practice" column. This column set out to be a vehicle for translating research and theory into classroom practice. Its intention was to provide a resource for middle school teachers of all subject areas with new and interesting ways to present their content to students of varied ability levels. I found out early in my career that it is difficult, if not impossible, to be a teacher with all of the before, during, and after-school responsibilities and be able to keep up with the current thinking in literacy. From that date on, the "Out of Research: Into Practice" column became a regular feature of the *Middle School Journal*.

In 1994, the columns were updated, edited, and published in a book by NMSA entitled, *Practical Strategies for Improving Instruction*. Since the column has continued throughout the last seven years, it seemed fitting to update and recast the book. Thus, this new book, *Strategies for Integrating Reading and Writing in Middle and High School Classrooms,* has emerged. This book is for teachers, administrators, teacher educators, and anyone else who wants to learn more about practical ways to integrate literacy across the content areas.

Joining me on this project is Dr. Janis Harmon, a former middle school reading teacher and currently an Associate Professor of Reading at the University of Texas San Antonio. Her expertise in content area literacy at the middle and secondary levels and her over 25 years in education adds a significant perspective to the book. Together we merged columns of similar topics, updated the research and current thinking, and expanded its scope to include teachers and their students in high schools. We have added many more classroom examples, some of which we either tried out ourselves or cited the accomplishments of teachers and students with whom we have worked. Among the subject areas examples included are the following: English/Language Arts, Mathematics/Algebra, Science/Chemistry, Social Studies/History, Health and Foreign Language.

With over 50 collective years of experience in education, our beliefs about how students learn are reflected in this book. We believe in inclusion, making sure that everyone, regardless of ability level, feels a part of what is going on in the classroom. Reflecting current and past research (Johnson & Johnson, 1991; Kagan, 1994; National Reading Panel, 2000; Slavin, 1995), we feel the best way to include all learners is through a model of collaborative learning in the form of flexible grouping. Many of the strategies presented in this book require that students help and assist one another, put their heads together, and jointly work toward a common goal or product.

As the title implies, this book is about integration, dissolving the boundaries between the subject areas and uniting them via literacy. Its main purpose is to improve students' understanding of content by increasing the amount of time they are engaged in actual reading and writing activities. We believe all classes should be reading and writing intensive and our beliefs are supported by the findings of the National Assessment of Educational Progress (U. S. Department of Education, 2000). Briefly stated, these findings indicate that the more time students spend engaged in reading and writing assignments whether for homework or class work, for pleasure or seeking information, the higher their achievement scores. Therefore, our main purposes in writing this book are to

- translate research and theory on literacy into classroom practice
- provide classroom teachers with a resource of strategies for improving students' performance and interest in course content
- provide concrete ways to incorporate reading and writing across all subject areas
- provide easy to read procedural guidelines to aid in classroom implementation
- illustrate each strategy with classroom examples, spanning all of the subject areas

The book contains 17 topic areas we loosely refer to as "chapters." Each chapter is based on a topic we know to be a need or an interest of middle and high school teachers. Within each chapter are several strategies, and along with each strategy are one or more sample lessons to illustrate the application to various subject areas. In most instances, the strategies are described in procedural, step-by-step detail. However, in some instances, a descriptive paragraph was sufficient for classroom implementation.

The chapters all follow the same four-part format.

- Research/Theory/Rationale. The "why" of the strategy or lesson. It gives teachers a brief overview of what the current thinking says on this topic and why it is important for students.
- Procedures/Description. The "how" of the strategy or lesson, either a detailed description or the step by step format on how to proceed to implement the strategy in a classroom is provided.
- Sample Lesson(s). The "what" of the strategy or lesson. It illustrates what it can look like in a classroom setting and shows ways it can be applied across subject areas and grade levels.
- References. The origin of the strategies as well as the citations of the research and theoretical support.

As co-authors, we still consider ourselves teachers first and foremost. So, fellow teachers, this one is for you!

KDW

JMH

References

Johnson, D. W., & Johnson, R. T. (1991) *Learning together and alone* (3rd edition). Boston: Allyn & Bacon.

Kagan, S. (1994) *Cooperative learning.* San Juan, CA: Kagan Cooperative Learning.

National Reading Panel (2000). *National reading panel report: Teaching children to read.* Bethesda, MD: Author. Retrieved June, 2001, from the World Wide Web: http://www.nationalreadingpanel.org/

Slavin, R. E. (1995). *Cooperative learning.* (2nd edition) Boston: Allyn & Bacon.

U.S. Department of Education, National Center for Education Statistics (2000). *The Condition of Education 2000*, NCES 2000-602. Washington, DC: U. S. Government Printing Office.

Wood, K.D. (1994). *Practical strategies for improving instruction.* Columbus, OH: National Middle School Association.

Foreword

What a pleasure it is for me to write a foreword for a text that is not only teacher-friendly, but also a valuable handbook for integrating literacy and learning in content areas throughout middle and high schools. The emphasis throughout this wonderful resource is on putting reading and writing to use as tools for learning. The implicit theories supporting the literacy strategies organized in this text are based on social constructivist theories of learning. That is to say, today's adolescents put reading and writing to good use in the classroom whenever they engage actively in a process of making sense and constructing meaning as they use text to learn. And students do this best within a cooperative and collaborative classroom that values social interaction, flexible grouping patterns, and cooperation.

Karen Wood and Janis Harmon underscore the belief that content area literacy has the potential to play an important role in the school lives of adolescents. Since the early 1900s a credible knowledge base has emerged, grounded in theory and research on the relationships between literacy and learning, to support the use of reading and writing strategies in all content areas. Wood and Harmon's text doesn't necessarily purport to teach reading and writing strategies in an explicit manner as reading teachers might do. While there is a convincing body of research that supports the role of "strategy instruction" in students' literacy development, there is an equally convincing body of research on the functional application of reading and writing strategies to support learning. A functional concept of content area reading came into prominence in the 1970s. Because functional instruction in content areas focuses on the integration of literacy strategies, classroom teachers are not placed in the position of believing that they are sacrificing an inordinate amount of instructional time to the explicit teaching of reading and writing. All too often in middle and high schools, explicit reading programs are limited to students who struggle with reading and writing. While these programs are valuable, all students need to be shown how to put reading and writing strategies to use. Here's where Wood and Harmon's book will help.

Throughout the past decade, the public discourse over literacy has focused primarily on the literacy learning of young children. One of the assumptions underlying early literacy policy is that once children learn to read, they will be able to use reading to learn for the rest of their lives. From a developmental perspective, such an assumption is faulty at best. The controversies over how young children learn to read and write serve only to magnify the lack of attention and commitment given to adolescent learners and their literacy needs. The literacy learning that takes place in adolescents between the ages of 10 and 18 is of critical importance in preparing for life in and out of school. As a society we can ill-afford to marginalize adolescent literacy at a time when the literacy development of young adolescents and teenagers is more critical than ever. Wood and Harmon provide middle and high school teachers with ready access to practical strategies that will make a difference in the school lives of adolescents.

I have always believed that content area literacy, with emphasis on the integration of reading and writing, is a matter of good teaching. Wood and Harmon believe this also. They select literacy strategies for emphasis that have been an integral part of their own teaching experiences. When these strategies are put into play teachers will be able to integrate reading, writing, and subject matter learning in seamless fashion, putting language and literacy to use to scaffold students' learning. Who could ask for anything more?

Richard T. Vacca
Kent State University
Past President, International Reading Association

1

Assessing the Literacy Abilities of Students Across the Subject Areas

Research/Theory/Rationale. Authentic assessment techniques play an important role in helping teachers determine student progress in all content areas. Traditional teacher-made tests with true-false statements and multiple choice items may not capture what students really know about the content being studied. This chapter describes three assessment practices, the *Content Inventory,* the *Free Association Assessment*, and *Techniques for Assessing Writing Performance.* The Content Inventory (Brozo & Simpson, 1995; Readence, Bean, & Baldwin, 1998; Vacca & Vacca, 1999) is an efficient means of determining which students can and cannot benefit from instruction in a subject area textbook. When used in conjunction with other evaluation devices, the inventory makes it possible to distinguish between inability and other causes for low performance throughout the school year. The Free Association Assessment helps teachers to create contexts that closely resemble how readers receive and store information in their minds by associating the new information with prior knowledge and experiences (McNeil, 1992). Finally, assessment of writing performance includes the use of teacher, peer, and self-assessment techniques.

CONTENT INVENTORY

The Content Inventory is a teacher-made diagnostic test administered to the class during the first week of school. Figure 1 (p. 3) is an example of a Content Inventory applied to social studies, and Figure 2 (p. 4) is an example applied to science. Content Inventories are based on the subject area textbook and are designed to assess student abilities in various areas. Some suggested categories for the inventory follow. *(The categories identified here are suggestions and are dependent on both subject matter and course objectives.)*

Knowledge of resources – The students respond to questions concerning their knowledge of library aids, based on what abilities the teacher determines are necessary for completing required course work.

Parts of the book – Students can use their book to demonstrate their knowledge of the table of contents, index, glossary, summary paragraphs, appendices, and other textbook aids.

Vocabulary – Questions can be asked to determine the students' general knowledge of the prefixes, suffixes, and roots common to a specific content area.

Additionally, words can be chosen from the text to determine if students can use context clues to arrive at the meaning of an unknown word.

Comprehension – The teacher should prepare the student to read a short selection by setting the purposes for reading and activating prior knowledge. Then, both literal and inferential questions should be asked to determine the extent to which the students understand the content of the passage.

Graphic aids – Students are asked to refer to specific pages in their textbook to determine their knowledge and ability to interpret charts, maps, graphs, and processes.

Developing the Inventory

- Examine your book and course objectives. Then develop categories (like the ones above) that are representative of the major skills needed to be successful in your course. Design five or more questions for each of the categories chosen.
- Develop questions for the comprehension section around a short selection of approximately three pages. It is often best to choose a passage from the beginning of the book before the information becomes too technical.
- Prepare copies of the inventory for the whole class. The inventory can be reused, since most textbooks are adopted for five years or longer. Also, inventories can be developed for other alternative material for classroom use.

Administering the Inventory

- Administer the inventory to the class during the first week of school. Explain to the students that this is an inventory of their skills, not a test or a graded assignment. An upbeat presentation should help to eliminate student anxiety or the need for collaboration.
- Go over the inventory and explain its components while students have a chance to see it. It may be helpful to read the questions orally before the students begin working on the inventory.
- Allow students to use their textbook for most of the answers, since one of the major purposes of the inventory is to ascertain their ability to read and use the book to complete required course work.

Scoring the Inventory

The inventory can be evaluated according to the following criteria.

- 90% or above correct: These students are reading the textbook at **their instructional level,** suggesting that with teacher guidance the students should be able to benefit from instruction with the text.
- 70% or below: Students scoring in this range are reading the text on **their frustration level** and will likely experience much difficulty handling the textbook. These students will need to be carefully observed doing other tasks to determine if additional testing is needed. They may need alternative materials, specialized assignments, or extensive textbook modification strategies to be successful.

FIGURE 1
Content Inventory Social Studies
Nations of the World

Directions: In most instances, you will use your book to answer the following questions. In some cases, you will be asked to draw upon your general knowledge of social studies. Remember, this is not a test and will not count as a grade. Instead, it is a way for me to determine how best to meet your needs. Do your very best, but don't worry if you do not know some answers.

I. Knowledge of Resources
1.   What is a biography? What is an autobiography?
2.   What library aid should be used to find out what resources are available on "Indochina?"
3.   If asked to do a research report on Napoleon Bonaparte, what resources would you use?
4.   Name a set of encyclopedias. Tell how the topics are arranged.
5.   If asked to do a report in class in which most of the information could be found in a magazine, what guide would tell you what magazine and issue to locate?

II. Parts of the Book
1.   In which chapter would you find information about Luxembourg?
2.   If you were asked to define the word *cuneiform,* where could you look first?
3.   What pages in the book would you look to find information about "aqueducts?" What textbook aid is used for this purpose?
4.   Look at the "Unit Preview" that precedes each unit.
     How does this help you in your study?
5.   On what page would you look to find a diagram of how silk was made? What textbook aid did you use?

III. Vocabulary
1.   Read the last paragraph in the first column on page 139. What are "junks?"
2.   Read the first column on page 135. What is meant by the "open-door policy?"
3.   What does the prefix "anti=" mean?
4.   Using your own background knowledge, define the following:
            monsoon • gondola • equator • nomad • guerilla
5.   Read the bottom of page 87 and describe an "obelisk" in your own words.

IV. Comprehension: Read pages 29-32 and answer the following questions.
1.   How long ago did man begin using fire?
2.   Explain the kind of rock that is best used for cutting.
3.   In what ways did early man's life-style change when he began to raise animals?
4.   Give some reasons why the number of people increased after the Ice Age.

V. Use of Maps, Charts, Diagrams, and Graphs
1.   Refer to the maps on pages 538 and 539. What changes took place in Africa from 1924-1968?
2.   Look at the graph on page 156. How many passenger cars were owned in Japan in 1976? How many television sets were owned in 1973?
3.   The diagram on page 124 tells how natural rubber is made. From what source do we get rubber? Briefly describe the first three steps.
4.   According to the product map on page 111, what area of India produces tea? Turn to the bar graph on page 332.
5.   Which country is the world's third largest producer of cheese? How many times greater is cheese production in the Soviet Union versus that of Italy?

FIGURE 2
Content Inventory: Science
Science Insights: Exploring Living Things

Directions: In most instances, you will use your book to answer the following questions. In some cases, you will be asked to draw upon your general knowledge of science. Remember, this is not a text and will not count as a grade. Instead, it is a way for me to determine how best to meet your needs. Do your very best, but don't worry if you do not know some answers.

I. **Knowledge of Resources**
    1. What is a search engine?
    2. Where would you first go on the Internet to find some information about fossils?
    3. If you had to research a major oil spill that occurred in the last ten years off the coast of Mexico, what books in the library would you use?
    4. Is there a section of the library for science books only?
    5. What magazines does the library have that deal with science?

II. **Parts of the Book**
    1. What section of Chapter 4 discusses cell theory?
    2. Where can you find a summary of Chapter 7?
        How is the format of the summary different from typical summaries?
    3. Look on page 341. What is the purpose of the numbers after the vocabulary words?
    4. On what page can you find information about kinds of infectious diseases?
    5. Where can you find the definition of *pathogen*? Is it defined in more than one place in the book?

III. **Vocabulary**
    1. Find "gastropods" on page 322. Define the term and give some examples.
    2. Read the second and third paragraphs on page 238 about nonvascular and vascular plants. What is the difference between the two plants? What word part helps you distinguish between the two?
    3. What part of the word "endoskeleton" helps you determine that the skeleton is inside the body?
    4. What word refers to the hard outer support structure of an arthropod?
    5. Using the information on page 517, how would you describe inflammation to someone?

IV. **Comprehension:** Read pages 444-449 to answer the following questions.
    1. List the parts of the nervous system.
    2. What is the function of each part?
    3. What part of the brain are you using to answer this inventory?
    4. How does an anesthetic help a person who is having an operation?
    5. How is CT imaging different from X-rays?

V. **Use of Maps, Charts, Diagrams, and Graphs**
    1. Using the table on page 125, what causes albinism?
    2. Read the table on page 177. What is the phylum of sunflowers?
    3. Examine the figure about lever systems on pages 404-405.
        What is the difference between a first-class lever and a third-class lever?
    4. Using the table on page 419, find out what causes an ulcer.
    5. Study the illustration of the brain (p. 446). What do you notice about the cerebellum?

The range between 70% and 90% correct is known as the **gray area.** Students scoring in this range will also need to be carefully monitored and may benefit from modification strategies as well

Developing a Class Profile

- A profile can be developed that indicates strengths and weaknesses for individual students and the class as a whole. (See Figure 3.)
- If a majority of students miss several items in a given area, the teacher may choose to revise course objectives or give extra emphasis to those areas. As another option, the teacher may choose to group students according to their instructional needs and provide additional assistance in areas of concern.

FIGURE 3
Content Inventory: Classroom Profile

Subject: Social Studies
Grade: 6

Period: 6
Date: September 2

Name	I. Knowledge of	II. Parts of Book	III. Vocabulary	IV Comprehension a. Literal	b. Inferential	Graphic Aids	Total Score	Comments
Kelly	-	+	-	+	+	+	87	
Ho Then	-	-	-	-	-	+	50	ESL student, attempted, responded well to help.
Tery	-	+	-	-	-	+	78	
Whitman	+	+	-	-	-	+	75	
Mike	+	+	+	-	-	-	85	
Tracie	+	+	-	+	+	+	90	
Betsy	+	+	-	-	-	+	82	
Ryan	-	+	+	+	+	-	80	
Millicent	-	-	-	-	-	+	63	
Stewart	-	-	-	-	-	+	70	Restless, would not stay in seat
Eric	+	+	+	+	+	-	95	Socializing with one another
Bart	+	+	-	+	+	+	95	Socializing with one another

FREE ASSOCIATIONAL ASSESSMENT

Free associational assessment (Wood, 1985; Griffin & Wood, 1995) enables teachers to assess how readers take in and store information associationally, by reconstructing meaning and making connections to experiences and knowledge already stored in their minds.

Procedures

- Compile a list of major concepts and important ideas to be taught and arrange the list in the order in which these concepts will be addressed in the textbook or class presentation. (See Figure 4.)
- Make copies of the list to distribute to students.
- Introduce each topic by setting a purpose for learning and by explaining that the list represents the important information that will be on the examination.
- Tell the students that the list can serve as a study guide for their test.

FIGURE 4

List of Major Concepts in Chapter 5, Lesson 1-2, "Matter"

Directions: Read lessons 1 and 2 in Chapter 5 (pp. 118-127). As you read, keep these key words and concepts in mind. You are encouraged to take notes (in your words) on a separate sheet. Soon after reading (within 24 hours) use this sheet to help you study and review the information. To begin with, look at each word and try to combine or associate all the information you can with it by thinking about it or quietly saying it to yourself. Continue this until you can successfully match the word with the correct information/definition. Soon after the reading and classroom experiments, you will be working with a partner in class and will participate in an "associational dialogue" pertaining to these concepts.

Matter
  Volume

States (of matter)
  Solid
  Liquid
  Gas
  Properties

Elements
  Atoms

Compounds
  Molecules
  Water

Mixtures
  Properties

Solutions
  Properties

- Encourage students to take notes on each topic during lectures, demonstrations, experiments, and while reading. Figure 5 (p. 7) shows an example of one student's notes on the topic of "matter." Students should take notes on a separate sheet of paper in order to use the list as a study prompt sheet.
- Explain that their notes should focus on key concepts and relevant details about the topic.
- Encourage students to review their notes within 24 hours of their reading and notetaking. Tell the students to read each item on the list and to associate as

---

FIGURE 5

Sample Student Cluster of Information for the Concept "Matter"

Matter – made up of atoms (really small – can't see them) all objects made of matter like our desks, stone walls

3 forms: solids (rocks)
           liquids (water)
           gasses (air)

Take up space

Einstein said matter can change

---

much information as possible by thinking about it or by sub-vocalizing the concepts.

- Allow the students to engage in an associational dialogue by working in pairs to actively discuss topics on the list using their own words.
- Then, begin a class discussion of the main ideas by asking questions and clarifying confusing ideas.
- Before taking the test, allow students to engage in another study session by reflecting on their collection of notes.
- Administer a nontraditional test consisting of a list of the major concepts. This is derived from the original list such as the one shown in Figure 4. Direct the students to write everything they can remember about each item listed by defining, providing examples, and showing how terms or ideas are related. Figure 6 (p. 8) illustrates the varying responses of four students who recalled everything they could remember on the topic of "elements." As can be seen, all of the responses to the free associational task reflect varying levels of understanding. Though different, both responses from students A and B are acceptable. Student A included a definition, examples, and extra details. Student B described the concept "elements" in terms less technical, putting the information in his/her own words. However, both students have a clear understanding of the term "elements." Student C, on the other hand, started off with an accurate definition of the concept, but added information that was incorrect and irrelevant. Student D only listed an example and did not offer further explanation of the concept.
- Grade the exam like an essay or open-ended exercise. For example, award a "+" for adequate response and a "-" for an insufficient answer. Another suggestion is to develop a rubric whereby points on a scale of 1 to 10 are awarded.
- After the grading, follow up by having students restudy those portions on which they received a negative evaluation, or provide alternative assignments to reinforce understanding and clear up misconceptions.

FIGURE 6
Sample Recalls on the Subtopic "Elements"

Student A: Elements are matter with only one kind of atom. Examples are: gold, silver, copper, and mercury. There are 109 elements on earth that scientists have found. My teacher said her bracelet was made of only one kind of atom (gold). The smaller whole bit of an element is an atom.

Student B: Elements have only one kind of material in them. A gold ring only has gold atoms in it. There are only 109 elements in the world.

Student C: Matter that only has one kind of atom is an element. It cannot take up space. It cannot be used to take up space or be used to do anything else. It can be used by one kind of atom.

Student D: Lead is an example of an element.

- Develop a class profile (see the partial class profile shown in Figure 7) with the major concepts listed across the top of the matrix and students' names down the side. This information will reveal what areas should be re-taught. In the hypothetical classroom shown in Figure 7, the teacher will certainly want to re-teach the topic of "compounds" and possibly group Eric, Jimmy, and Michelle for additional study of "mixtures."

FIGURE 7
Partial Class Profile Unit: "Matter"

Students' Names	Matter	Compounds	Elements	Mixtures
1. Kevin	+	-	+	+
2. Lauren	+	-	+	+
3. Ryan	-	+	+	+
4. Eric	+	-	+	-
5. Jimmy	+	-	+	-
30. Michelle	+	-	+	-

ASSESSING WRITING PERFORMANCE

As students engage in the writing process, teachers need to consider realistic and effective ways to assess student progress in their writing. Because many writing assignments are practice efforts, it is not necessary to grade every written product. When the teacher feels it is necessary to finalize a first draft or turn a paper in for credit, a number of assessment strategies can be employed, including checkpoint scales for teacher assessment, peer assessment, and self-assessment (Wood, 1994).

Teacher Assessment
Checkpoint Scales

Procedures
- Develop the criteria for a Checkpoint Scale (Kirby & Liner, 1981) as depicted in Figure 8 (p. 11). The criteria should coordinate with specific curricular objectives, making the scale reflect subject area content and/or technical objectives (e.g., grammar, punctuation, coherence, etc.).
- Multiply students' scores on each criteria by a number (listed at the end of the line in the example) depending on how much weight is allotted to each element.
- For the "Overall Impression" element, provide students with a general opinion of the composition similar to holistic scoring. Give the overall numerical grade and comments you write to the students to help them locate, revise, and repair any areas of need.

Peer Assessment

Peer editing is a timesaving way to evaluate writing assessment by involving students in the process. Students learn from both the writing and the editing process as they analyze their drafts for needed revisions in content and mechanics.

Determining Groups

Procedures
- Engage students in peer editing by asking them to choose a partner or by pre-assigning students to partners or small groups.
- Model the kinds of things students can look for and say when they are critiquing another's paper. This can be done by displaying via an overhead or reading aloud a teacher-developed example which needs revision and then "talking aloud" with the aid of the class about the strengths and weaknesses.
- Consider the following instructional sequence recommended by Harp and Brewer (1991):
  —Members take turns reading aloud their compositions to the group.
  —Group members then name at least one thing they liked about the manuscript.
  —Group members make one or more suggestions for improvement. For example, "I really got excited when you described the ghost, but before that, it dragged a little. Maybe you could start with your second paragraph and leave off the first details."
  —The student author makes notes from the group members' comments for later revision.
  —Two group members exchange papers to read the composition for changes in punctuation, grammar, and/or spelling.

Scan Scoring

Scan scoring is an assessment technique which begins with peer editing and culminates with the teacher's evaluative comments (described by Wood, 1987). The peer editing form for "Point of View" writing can be used generically in any subject area (see Figure 9, p. 12). The criteria to be examined can also be changed to coordinate with the writing assignment and specific class objectives.

Procedures

- Preassign students to groups of four or five members and give each student specific role assignments about what to critique. The role assignments can be determined by the teacher or the group members. As illustrated in Figure 9, each member in this group reads the paper for one of the following: beginning, middle, end, run-on sentences, sentence fragments, or spelling.
- Direct students to revise their drafts at this stage according to the comments of their peers or have them turned in for further teacher evaluation.
- Using the Scoring Form illustrated in Figure 10 (p. 13); scan the compositions and peer editing responses first before asking the students to make revisions. The grading scale can be modified to coordinate with teacher expectations and goals.

Self-Assessment

Self-assessment is an important aspect of the writing process, because it helps students develop independence and self-reliance as they engage in different writing tasks. Self-assessment can be conducted in rough drafts or in the completed composition stage.

Procedures

- Devise a checklist (Tompkins, 1990) for students to use in assessing the quality of their rewriting and to determine whether they have met the requirements set forth by the teacher (see Figure 11, p. 13).
- Make copies of the checklist or write it on the board or an overhead transparency.
- Review the boldface words to ensure that the students fully understand the elements to be included.
- Adapt the checklist according to topic, subject area, grade, and ability level.
- Ask students to complete the second self-evaluation form on mechanics as illustrated in Figure 12 (p. 14). This checklist requires students to focus on individual errors and encourages more careful proofreading of written assignments (Wood, 1987). Students indicate the area in need of change with a minus and then they circle it after making the corrections.

FIGURE 8
Checkpoint Scales

Your revised draft on   *Descriptive writing*
       "My room and what's in it."
received the following rating:

Name   *Ryan*
Date   *February 14*
Grade   *8*

Organization (beginning, middle, and end)

1	2	3	4	5	X4=*12*
I had a lot of trouble following your plan. Rethink your outline and try to tighten this up.		You're on the right track, but it's still hard to follow your plan.		Great organization. I was right with you.	

Details (reasons, elaboration)

1	2	3	4	5	X4=*20*
You didn't give enough information. Be more specific but stay away from lists.		There are some good ideas here. You need to tell your reader a little more.		Good vivid details. I get the picture.	

Mechanics (proofing)

1	2	3	4	5	X3=*6*
Can't tell what you're trying to say with all the errors. Try again.		A few errors got by you this time. See if you can find them.		What a proofreader! You really have an eye for that job.	

Overall Impression

1	2	3	4	5	X5=*20* TOTAL=*58*
You could do much more with this assignment. Return to the prewriting outline and start again.		The potential is there. With a little more effort you'll have it.		What a pleasure to read. You composed a fine piece of writing.	

Comments

Ryan, you are such a creative thinker. I love your descriptions! Rework that last paragraph. I had trouble following your ideas in the end. Also, be sure to proofread (especially punctuations). After that, you'll have a great composition.

FIGURE 9
Peer Editing Form

Point of View
(Type of Writing)

"Let's Save the Animals"
(Assignment Title)

Name   *Ryan*
Date   *February 14*
Class *Mrs. Spear*
Grade *7*

Author   *Kevin M*

Editor   *Ryan*
Criteria *Beginning*

Telling about the pandas and dolphins first was a good idea. It made me want to help right away.

Author   *Kevin M*

Editor   *Myron*
Criteria *Middle/End*

The middle is hard to understand, but the ending is pretty good.

Author   *Kevin M*

Editor   *Mandy*
Criteria *Run-on sentences/fragments*

Look at the middle paragraph. I think you have some sentence fragments.

Author   *Kevin M*

Editor   *Sarah Ann*
Criteria *Spelling*

I circled the spelling errors I noticed.

FIGURE 10
Teacher Scoring Form

Score results for:

Point of View

"Let's Save the Animals"

(Assignment Title)

Name	*Kevin Michael*
Date	*December 2*
Class	*Language Arts, Social Studies*
Grade	*7*

Content Criteria
   good beginning
   middle needs work
   good ending

Proofing Criteria
   sentence fragments
   spelling

Grade Scale

A = all 3 content criteria and no proofing errors

B = all 3 content criteria with errors

C = two of the three content criteria, no proofing errors

D = two of the three content areas with proofing errors

E = not enough content for assignment proofing credit

Initial Grade   *B*   Final Grade   ———

Comments: *Kevin, your beginning and ending convinced me to save the animals. The middle paragraphs are confusing. Clear up those spelling errors and you'll have an A+ paper.*

FIGURE 11
Self-evaluation: Content
(modified by Tompkins, 1990)

Name *Lauren*   **Country** *Spain*

After writing your draft, be certain you have included the following information:

Yes	No	
✓		Have you written information about the geography of the country?
	✓	Have you drawn a map of the country?
✓		Have you written information about the history of the country?
✓		Hav you described the topography of the country?
	✓	Have you written information about the economy of the country?
✓		Have you written information about the natural resources of the country?
✓		Have you written information about the climate of your country?
✓		Have you written something special about the country?
✓		Have you included information that you requested about your country?

Briefly tell what your project plans are:

I plan on doing a skit with Kevin, Ryan, and Sarah Ann on bullfighting. Then I will have the class share their opinions in a panel discussion.

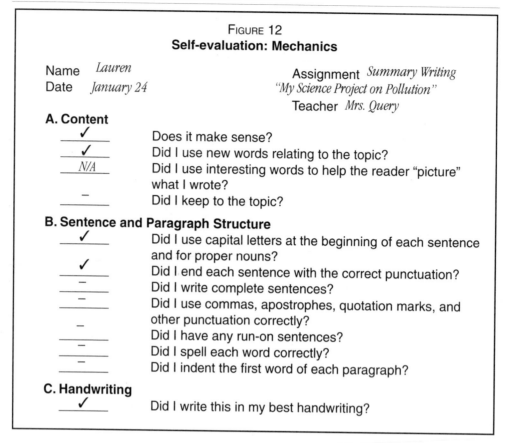

FIGURE 12
Self-evaluation: Mechanics

Name   *Lauren*   Assignment   *Summary Writing*
Date   *January 24*   *"My Science Project on Pollution"*
                                              Teacher   *Mrs. Query*

A. Content

✓	Does it make sense?
✓	Did I use new words relating to the topic?
N/A	Did I use interesting words to help the reader "picture" what I wrote?
−	Did I keep to the topic?

B. Sentence and Paragraph Structure

✓	Did I use capital letters at the beginning of each sentence and for proper nouns?
✓	Did I end each sentence with the correct punctuation?
−	Did I write complete sentences?
−	Did I use commas, apostrophes, quotation marks, and other punctuation correctly?
−	Did I have any run-on sentences?
−	Did I spell each word correctly?
−	Did I indent the first word of each paragraph?

C. Handwriting

✓	Did I write this in my best handwriting?

References

Brozo, W. G., & Simpson, M. L. (1995). *Readers, teachers, and learners: Expanding literacy in secondary schools.* Englewood Cliffs, NJ: Merrill.

Harp, B., & Brewer, J. A. (1991) *Reading and writing: Teaching for the connections.* New York: Harcourt, Brace Jovanovich.

Kirby, D., & Liner, T. (1981). *Inside out: Developmental strategies for teaching writing.* Montclair, NJ: Boynton/Cook.

Griffin, W. B., & Wood, K. D. (1995). Free associational assessment is another alternative way to test. *Middle School Journal, 26* (4), 65-68.

McNeil, J. D. (1992). *Reading comprehension: New directions for classroom practice.* New York: HarperCollins.

Readence, J. B., Bean, T. W., & Baldwin, R. S. (1998). *Content area literacy: An integrated approach.* Dubuque, IA: Kendall/Hunt

Tompkins, G.E. (1990). *Teaching writing: Balancing process and product.* Columbus, OH: Merrill.

Vacca, R. T., & Vacca, J. L. (1999). *Content area reading: Literacy and learning across the curriculum.* (6th ed.). New York: Longman.

Wood, K. D. (1985). Free associational assessment: An alternative to traditional testing. *Journal of Reading, 29* (2), 106-110.

Wood, K. D. (1987). Evaluating progress in the language arts. In C. R. Personke & D. D. Johnson (Eds.), *Language arts instruction and the beginning teacher* (pp. 330-332). Englewood Cliffs, NJ: Prentice-Hall.

Wood, K. D. (1994). *Practical strategies for improving instruction.* Columbus, OH: National Middle School Association.

2

Meeting the Cognitive and Affective Needs of Middle and High School Students Through Cooperative Learning

Research/Theory/Rationale. According to Johnson, Johnson, and Holubec (1993), cooperative learning is "the instructional use of small groups so that students work together to maximize their own and each other's learning" (p. 6). This collaboration provides students with opportunities for learning that may not be achieved by working individually. Research studies indicate that social interactions influence reading strategies (Wilkinson & Silliman, 2000). For example, Almasi and Gambrell (1994) noted better results in learning with student-directed groups instead of teacher-directed groups. The call for more cooperative learning arrangements is especially critical in middle and secondary classrooms where the social needs of students impact their development and learning. Alvermann et al. (1996) found that collaborative group work enhanced learning when adolescents worked with others who shared their same beliefs about learning. Active participation in group activities enables students at this level to develop a stronger self-esteem, to engage in positive group interactions, and to increase academic learning (Vacca & Vacca, 1999). Because peer interaction is a driving force that motivates adolescents (Irvin, 1998), this propensity for social engagement can be useful in configuring effective learning environments for adolescents. A variety of cooperative learning arrangements that are easily implemented and appropriate for all subject areas are described here (Wood, 1987).

GROUP RETELLINGS

One method of ensuring class-wide participation is through the use of group retellings. In this approach students work in pairs or in groups of three or more with each member reading either a. the same material, such as from a basal reader, literature anthology, or content area textbook; b. a different type of topically-related material as a brochure, encyclopedia excerpt, or news article; or c. material written at different grade levels but related to the topic under study. In the latter example of group retellings, the teacher, using a flexible grouping model, would assign students to reading groups based on their proficiency. This would allow less skilled readers the opportunities to read selections more suited to their ability levels and subsequently participate in whole class discussions and assignments. Below is a sample classroom scenario of group retellings used with a lesson on health or science. Figure 1 (p. 16) illustrates the use of group retellings with a mathematics lesson.

Science or Health Example

- Select three varied texts on the topic of the cardiovascular system. One piece of material might be a brochure from the local health department on recognizing a heart attack; another could be an excerpt from an informational book on the heart; and yet another could be a passage taken from a website on the Internet.
- Assign each student in the group to read one of the texts. Remind them that they are responsible for retelling it in their own words to other group members.
- Encourage group members to interject with related information from their own readings or past experiences.
- At various points in the lesson, have the groups share what they have read with the entire class.
- Individualize this group activity by assigning shorter, easier material to the less able students.

FIGURE 1
Group Retellings
Mathematics—Sample Transcript
Decimals

Problem: 3.15 x .75=

Student A: First, we need to line up the numbers so we can multiply, without getting mixed up.
    3.15
    x.75

Student B: Then we start at the right and multiply like we usually would. Don't worry about the decimal right now.

Student C: 5 times 5 is 25. The 5 goes under the 5's on the right and we carry the 2. Then multiply 5 x 1 which is 5, then add 2.

Student A: That's 7. And 5 x 3 is 15. That's 1575.

Student B: The next row moves over to the left one space. I get 2205. How about everybody else?

Student C: That's it. Now we add (pointing). Bring down the 5; 7 plus 5 is 12, carry the 1; 1 plus 5 is 6, 1 plus 2 is 3, and bring down the 2. That's 23625.

Student A: What about the decimal point?

Student B: Count the total number of digits to the right of the decimal in the problem—it's 4. Then start at the right of the answer and count 4 digits. The decimal goes to the left of the 4th digit.

Student C: So the answer is 2.3625!

BUDDY SYSTEM GROUPING

The buddy system approach (Fader, 1976), as the name implies, involves grouping students of varied abilities and making them responsible for each other's learning. Differences in ability levels are minimized to avoid both boredom and intimidation.

Yet, the differences are still sufficient to ensure that they can benefit from each other's experiences.

Procedures
- Rearrange the class role from the "most prepared" to the "least prepared."
- Divide the class list into three even divisions.
- To form 10 heterogeneous groups, select the top names from each division to form one group. Then, the number 2 students from each division form another group, and the number 3 students from each division form another until the last group would be composed of the last member of each of the three divisions.
- Because they are responsible for each other's learning, inform group members that they must check each other's work and offer assistance before turning in any assignments.

RESEARCH GROUPING

At any stage of the instructional lesson, before, during, or after the reading, students can work in groups to investigate an issue in more depth. Whether the choice is laboratory research involving actual scientific experiments or library research for the purpose of solving unanswered questions, research grouping is an excellent method to employ. For example, a social studies class may be divided into groups to gather more information on Civil War battles, generals, or everyday life. Groups in a health class may seek varied sources to find more information on poison control or childhood diseases. When employing research grouping, it is helpful to give students a collaborative sequence to follow with roles and tasks assigned to each group member.

Collaborative Sequence
- Students in each group take on the responsibility of searching various sources, either encyclopedias, books, pamphlets, magazines, websites, or CD ROMs for information on the topic.
- The group members decide how to synthesize the sources.
- One group member serves as a recorder or scribe while the group members create a rough draft of their synthesis about the topic.
- The group members then reread what they have written, making necessary revisions.
- The group members become editors, reading the paper for mechanical and content modifications. A second recorder or scribe can make these revisions.

The illustration in Figure 2 (p. 18) shows how this process can be depicted in abbreviated format to aid groups in understanding their roles and meeting their objectives. Ideally, this sequence, or one similar, should be written on the board or a poster and explained thoroughly prior to the lesson.

Figure 2
Reading Group Assignments

Each member: Assign research roles—information books, websites on the Internet, encyclopedias, magazines; take notes to share with group
Entire group: Combine notes; share ideas for synthesis
Individual: First recorder writes ideas of the group
Entire group: Read and revise paper
Individual: Second recorder makes revisions
Each member: Assign editorial roles – grammar, punctuation, sentence structure, content
Entire group: Final copy reading and revision

Cybernetic Sessions

Masztal (1986) developed cybernetic sessions in which small groups of students respond to predetermined questions during a specified period of time. Cybernetic sessions can be used before a new lesson as a means of eliciting students' prior experiences with a topic. Or, they can be used after a lesson as a form of review. Procedures for the four phases of cybernetic sessions follow.

Preplanning Phase
- Select thought-provoking questions from any subject area, such as questions about the digestive system in science, literary elements of a novel, or every-day uses of the decimal system in mathematics. The questions need to elicit much discussion and interaction.
- Write each question on a separate poster board and hang the boards around the classroom to form question stations.

Response Generating Phase
- Assign students to groups of four or five and ask them to sit around each of the question stations.
- Instruct students to write down on a separate sheet of paper as many responses as possible to the given question. One student can serve as recorder for the question.
- At the end of the allotted time, direct students to move on to the next question station.
- Instruct students to repeat the process of writing down as many responses to the question as they can on another sheet of paper. A different student can serve as a recorder for each question.
- Direct students to complete all question stations in the same manner.

Data Synthesis Phase
- Conduct a whole class discussion so that the students can hear the responses of all their classmates.
- Write the various answers under each posted question or ask a student to be the scribe.
- Continue the whole class discussion emphasizing new concepts and ideas.

Final Presentation Phase
- Place the completed posters on the bulletin board so students can reread them later for review purposes.
- Type the information as handouts for the students to use as study guides.

TUTORIAL GROUPING

When students are in need of assistance, tutorial grouping is the next best alternative to direct teacher-to-student interaction. In tutorial grouping, two students work together and are responsible for each other's learning. As such, the disparity between them should not be so great as to intimidate a partner. Likewise, pairs should not be so similar in terms of ability that they are unable to aid each other's progress. Learning or reading disabled, ESL, or educable mentally handicapped students are often unable to handle grade level material. Therefore, the teacher may choose to assign the majority of the class the textbook reading while tutorial groups work in topically related alternative materials written at an easier grade level.

A useful management device for tutorial grouping is the lesson plan form shown in an excerpted form in Figure 3. This form is filled out initially by the teacher and then later taken over by the tutor and tutee as more responsibility is allotted to them.

Tutorial grouping is most effective when it is not used excessively. Otherwise, the chosen students may feel isolated from their classmates. When deemed necessary, the teacher may say something like, "For the first half of the period, form your tutorial groups and begin your next assignment. The remainder of the class will work in pairs on the textbook assignment. I will be around to assist all of you. Then, we will all see a demonstration on insect life."

FIGURE 3
Excerpt from Lesson Plan Form

Names: John/Doug
Subject: Science

Date	What I plan to do today	What I did today
9/4	Read *Gateways to Science,* pages 24-27 with partner. Write down 10 new ideas.	I finished reading and wrote down five ideas. Doug wrote 3 more.
9/6	Study display case on insects in room with partner. Choose 3 insects. Write 3 facts about each from *Gateways,* Chapter 2.	I chose spiders, roaches, and flies. I wrote my facts from the book.

INTEREST GROUPING

Capitalizing on the specific interests of adolescents is often a sure-fire way to motivate them to undertake an assignment. After the introduction of a particular unit in any subject area, the teacher can provide a list of activity or content-based choices. Some content-based choices in social studies, for example, may include collecting more information and objects related to Greece including food, climate, dress, and government. Other activity-based choices might involve presenting a skit, making a demonstration, engaging a speaker, developing a project, or writing a report.

DYADIC LEARNING

Larson and Dansereau (1986) recommend having students work in dyads (pairs) to study their subject area assignments.

Procedures
- One student reads a segment (from a paragraph up to two pages) of the textbook or assigned selection.
- The other partner assumes the role of "listener/facilitator" by correcting errors, adding information, or clarifying concepts.
- Both students work together to draw charts, maps, outlines, graphs, pictures, or other visual representations that will further their understanding and recall of what was read.
- After each segment is read and discussed, the partners switch roles for the next segment.
- At any point in the lesson, the teacher may call for a class-wide discussion of the textbook concepts.

ASSOCIATIONAL DIALOGUE

The associational dialogue is a component of a strategy called free associational assessment (Wood, 1985; Griffin & Wood, 1995) that uses students' free recalls as a means of evaluation. The dialogue portion can be used separately as an aid to the oral review process.

Procedures
- Prepare a list of the most significant concepts in the lesson to be taught.
- Direct students to take notes of these concepts from class demonstrations and the textbook until they have "associational clusters" of relevant infor- mation. See the example in Figure 4 (p. 21) and notice how both student A and B are discussing/studying/reviewing (using a conversational style) the information on which they took "clusters" of notes.

- Encourage students to use information from their own experiences to further assist in retention.
- Tell students to look at the unmarked, original list of concepts and to mentally or subvocally recite as much of the associated content they can recall.
- Encourage students to continue this recitation until they feel they can comfortably associate the word with the related content.
- Provide class time for students to work in pairs, engaging in the associational dialogue by discussing each concept in their own words.
- Circulate among the pairs clarifying important terms and providing further information.
- After the student dialogue reviews, discuss selected concepts with the whole class, eliciting student contributions, and filling in gaps where needed.

FIGURE 4
Example of Associational Dialogue

The Mountain West States: Land and Climate
List of concepts, places, people
timberline
Contintental Divide
arroyo
semidesert
rain shadow

Student Free Recalls of "Associational Clusters"
"Continental Divide"

Student A —   An imaginary line like the Prime Meridian, but it's located in the Rockies. It divides the flow of rivers. Rivers on the east side flow east. Rivers on the west side flow west. On our trip out west, people called it the Great Divide.

Student B —   The Continental Divide determines which way rivers will flow. The Snake River, on the west side, flows west. The Yellowstone River, on the east side, flows east. The Blue River, near us, must flow to the east because it is east of the Continental Divide.

GENERAL LESSON GROUPING

Described by Nelson-Herber (1988), the General Lesson Grouping is a method for grouping that is appropriate for a variety of purposes. In this form of grouping, the teacher assigns roles to each group member before the lesson proceeds. Roles such as *checker* and *encourager* ensure that compassion is shown for fellow students and that no one's needs are overlooked.

Procedures

- Begin by asking students to move into groups of five and to write down as many words they can think of about the specified topic.
- Assign a *recorder* for each group to write down the contributed words or phrases.
- Allow the groups to share their contributions with the whole class and then conduct a discussion about how each word relates to the topic.
- As a class, construct a graphic organizer or web using the words elicited by the groups. Make sure the visual representation shows the relationships between key concepts.
- Using categories from the graphic organizer, ask the students to make predictions about the selection before beginning to read.
- Have students answer 5-6 questions about the selection in their group as they read. Designate a leader to read the questions and start the reading and searching process. At this point, more proficient readers can assist less able readers with difficult words and concepts.
- Direct the *recorder* of the group to write down the answers as a *checker* ensures that everyone understands the answers. The *encourager* makes sure that all group members have a chance to participate.
- Circulate among the groups, answering questions and providing assistance or supervision when needed.
- Conduct a whole class discussion about the answers to the questions.

RANDOM GROUPING

In some instances, it may be necessary to group students randomly. Merely directing the students to "pair up with someone seated near you" or "get into groups of four" can make the math word problems or the science textbook questions more understandable to more students. Another way of randomizing students is to have them count off by 2's, 3's, or 4's depending on the group size needed.

BASE GROUPING

Johnson and Johnson (1985) have found what they call base or home groups very useful. Students within a class are assigned to a base or a home group at the beginning of the year. Then, when deemed necessary, usually 5 or 10 minutes before the beginning of the lesson, the teacher calls the students into their base groups. Here, they have the opportunity to greet classmates, discuss the previous night's homework, confer on a project, or relate an anecdote relevant to an assignment. This procedure begins the class on a positive note since it allows students an opportunity to informally interact with their peers on academic matters.

NEEDS GROUPING

Sometimes it is necessary to group students according to their strengths and weaknesses in a particular area. Unless the teacher has a systematic plan for ongoing assessment, these needs can go unnoticed until the first test or even later. Two methods for determining students' needs are 1) pre- and post- testing, and 2) arranging assessment tests topically.

Pre- and Post- Testing. Pretests can be developed before teaching a unit on grammar, for example, to determine students' knowledge of comma usage, end-of-sentence punctuation, or rules of capitalization. Similarly, they can be used to pre-assess students' understanding of math concepts and computations. In this way, the teacher can eliminate the teaching of unnecessary material and find out who has specific needs. Post-tests can be used after the instructional lesson to ascertain who has or has not mastered particular skills or concepts.

Assessment of Topics. By arranging chapter or unit tests topically, the teacher can evaluate what students have learned and what they still need to know. By using a grid such as the one shown below, the teacher can judge if additional explanation of concepts is needed for the entire class or for specific students. The teacher can use a simple + if the majority of the items on a particular topic were mastered or a – if they were not. As the grid in Figure 5 indicates, the students profiled could be grouped for more instruction in "causes of" and "controlling" pollution, which are the weakest areas. Another possibility is to have students who performed better on the test explain the concepts to those whose test performance suggests a lack of understanding.

	FIGURE 5						
	Partial Class Profile						
	Science Unit: Environmental Pollution						
Student's Name	Air	Water	Soil	Noise	Solid Water	Causes	Controling
1. Ryan	+	+	+	+	+	-	+
2. Eric	+	+	-	-	-	+	-
3. Sherry	+	-	-	+	-	-	-
4. Tara	+	+	-	+	-	-	-
30.							

APPLYING COOPERATIVE LEARNING ACROSS THE SUBJECT AREAS

Figure 6 (p. 24) illustrates how many of the strategies discussed in this chapter can be applied to all subject areas in any given week. The implementation of cooperative learning techniques requires school-wide training and commitment to ensure success.

FIGURE 6

A Sample Weekly Schedule for Grouping in All Subject Areas

	MONDAY	TUESDAY	WEDNESDAY	THURSDAY	FRIDAY
LANGUAGE ARTS/ ENGLISH	Introduce point-of-view paragraph writing Assignment— Model for whole class	Students work in buddy system groups to compose and edit.	Students are paired randomly to compose a single descriptive paragraph	Students work individually and then share compositions with original Buddy System Group for editing	Students volunteer individual efforts with Whole Class Work displayed
SOCIAL STUDIES	Teacher builds background on "India." Whole class.	Group retellings of varied, topically-related material.	Students begin Interactive Reading Guide on textbook chapter.	Students continue Interactive Reading Guide	Teacher and students pose topics for future Interest Groups
SCIENCE	Demonstration on "Source of Pollution." Whole class.	Students read relevant textbook section. Dyadic learning.	Whole class discussion of textbook content.	Students choose related topics—form Research Groups	Research Groups continue
MATH	Teacher models use of percentages on overhead. Whole class.	Students practice in pairs. Tutorial grouping.	Students practice individually	Progress test given	Students grouped according to need

References

Almasi, J., & Gambrell, L. (1994). *Sociocognitive conflict in peer-led and teacher-led discussions of literature* (Rep. No. 12). University of Maryland and University of Georgia, National Reading Research Center. University of Georgia.

Alvermann, D., Young, J., Weaver, D., Hinchman, K., Moore, D., Phelps, S., Thrash, S., & Zalewkis, E. (1996). Middle and high school students' perceptions of how they experience text-based discussions: A multicase study. *Reading Research Quarterly, 31,* 244-267.

Fader, D. (1976). *The new hooked on books.* New York: Berkley.

Griffin, W. B., & Wood, K. D. (1995). Free associational assessment is another alternative method for testing. *Middle School Journal, 26* (4), 65-68.

Irvin, J. L. (1998). *Reading and the middle school student: Strategies to enhance literacy* (2nd ed.). Boston: Allyn & Bacon.

Johnson, R. T., & Johnson, D. W. (1985). Student-student interaction: Ignored but powerful. *Journal of Teacher Education, 36,* 22-26.

Johnson, D. W., Johnson, R. T., & Holubec, E. J. (1993). *Circles of learning: Cooperation in the classroom* (4th ed.). Edina, MN: Interaction Book Company.

Larson, C. O., & Dansereau, D. E. (1984). Cooperative learning in dyads. *Journal of Reading, 27,* 458-460.

Masztal, N.B. (1986). Cybernetic sessions: A high involvement teaching technique. *Reading Research and Instruction, 25,* 131-138.

Nelson-Herber, J. (1988). Cooperative learning: Research into practice. *Reading Journal, 5,* 16.

Vacca, R. T., & Vacca, J. L. (1999). *Content area reading: Literacy and learning across the curriculum* (6th ed.). New York: Longman.

Wilkinson, L. C., & Silliman, E. R. (2000). Classroom language and literacy learning. In M. L. Kamil, P. B. Mosenthal, P. D. Pearson, & R. Barr (Eds.), *Handbook of reading research: Volume III* (pp. 337-360). Mahwah, NJ: Erlbaum.

Wood, K. D. (1985). Free associational assessment: An alternative to traditional testing. *Journal of Reading, 19,* 106-111.

Wood, K. D. (1987). Fostering cooperative learning in middle and secondary level classrooms. *Journal of Reading, 13,* 10-18.

Improving Reading and Writing Through Group Participation

Research/Theory/Rationale. Data from the National Assessment of Educational Progress in Reading (Donahue, Voelkl, Campbell, & Mazzeo, 1999) as well as other sources (Calkins, 1994) reveal to us that the more time students spend in reading and writing, the greater their level of achievement. We also know that middle and high school students benefit from the social interactions of working in groups (Vacca & Vacca, 1999; Wilkinson & Silliman, 2000). This chapter describes several approaches that encourage group participation for both reading and writing. The Guided Reading Procedure enables teachers to capitalize on the varied backgrounds and experiences of the students by using "collective recalls" of the class as a whole. The teaching approaches for incorporating writing with subject matter learning are based on the communal writing concept whereby small groups of students work together to develop a single composition between them.

GUIDED READING PROCEDURE

The Guided Reading Procedure or GRP (Manzo, 1975; Manzo, Manzo, & Estes, 2001) uses student input as a means of communicating the content of instructional material. It is an appropriate strategy for all subject areas and tasks, including math word problems and following directions. Although described here in conjunction with reading, the steps can be applied to listening or viewing and require minimal preparation time for teachers. The most outstanding feature of the Guided Reading Procedure is that all students, regardless of ability level, can make a contribution to the class with minimal risk. Since adolescents are particularly sensitive to taking social risks, it is rewarding to see them eager to contribute a word or phrase even when they are not called on to do so.

Procedures
- Conduct the pre-reading phase of the lesson by building background knowledge, pre-teaching vocabulary, relating the new topic to the students' pre-existing knowledge, and setting purposes for reading.
- After the pre-reading introduction to the lesson, tell the students that their purpose is to read and remember all they can about the assigned selection. The selection is usually limited to no more than two to five pages of topically related information.

- With their books closed, ask the class to recall anything they can about the selection just read. Not being able to look back in the text forces the students to actively retrieve the information from memory resulting in a mental or vocal recitation of the content.
- Write the "collective recalls" of the class on the board or on a transparency in the order given. Conclude this step when the class can no longer recall any more information or whenever it is deemed appropriate to move on to the next step. (See Figure 1, p. 28).
- Have the students skim the selection to determine if any significant information has been left out.
- Work together with the students to reorganize the information. It is recommended that the reorganization step follow the structure of the materials and may be in (a) sequential order as with narrative materials or events, (b) cause and effect, or (c) main idea with supporting details, to name a few.
- During the reorganization and afterwards, begin asking probing questions that will help students reflect on and make inferences about the content.
- As an optional follow-up activity, give the students a test to determine their short-term memory for the concepts discussed.
- Another option is to have the class use the ordered concepts as a basis for writing about the new information learned (see Section III in Figure 1). The key concepts/phrases now organized according to the original text provide an excellent opportunity to integrate writing as a class, in small groups, pairs, or individually.

COMMUNAL WRITING

Communal writing (Wood, 1994) is an expedient way to help students become better writers by practicing the process of writing. Students are pre-assigned to groups of four or five with each group becoming a community of writers who work together, contribute ideas, and assist one another. Requiring a single composition from each group alleviates the "I can't get started because I don't know what to write" or "blank page syndrome." It also serves to contain the unfocused writer who tends to write pages of disconnected and detailed content. Three strategies for incorporating communal writing across the curriculum are described next: exchange compare writing, story impressions, and capsule vocabulary.

EXCHANGE COMPARE WRITING

Exchange Compare Writing (Wood, 1986) requires that students predict the content of a selection from key vocabulary terms presented in random order. Students can then compose a different passage, after reading, based upon the new information learned in the selection.

Figure 1
Sample Lesson Using the Guided Reading Procedure
The Civil War in the East, 1861-1864

I. **The Collective Recalls of the Students**
- Beauregard attacked Fort Sumter
- Jackson named "Stonewall"
- Battles have two names
- Bull Run
- Manassas
- Fort Sumter
- Creek named Bull Run
- Appalachian Mountains
- Poorly-trained volunteers
- No planning strategy
- April 12, 1861
- Union army under General McDowell
- Confederates confident
- McDowell attacked
- Beauregard's forces

II. **The Collective Reorganization of the Information**
- Appalachian Mountains divided eastern and western wars
- No prepared strategy
- Poorly-trained volunteers

Fort Sumter
- Began April 12, 1861
- Beauregard and Confederates attacked Fort Sumter
- Charleston Harbor, SC

First Bull Run or Manassas
- Battles have two names
- Confederates named them after settlements
- Northerners named them after bodies of water
- Creek named Bull Run
- Union army under General McDowell
- McDowell attacked Beauregard
- Jackson named "Stonewall"
- Union force fled
- Confederates confident

III. **Summary**
The battles fought during the Civil War occurred on the east and west side of the Appalachian Mountains. Two major battles on the east side were Fort Sumter and Bull Run. The Civil War began with Beauregard leading the Confederate attack on Fort Sumter in Charleston Harbor, South Carolina, on April 12, 1861. The Confederates easily took control of Fort Sumter. The confederates also won another battle, called Bull Run by the Northerners and Manassas by the Confederates. The Confederates named battles after settlements and the Northerners named them after bodies of water. Bull Run was a creek that ran by Manassas. McDowell, the leader of the Union army, attacked the Confederates who were led by General Beauregard and Stonewall Jackson. The Confederates were confident and forced the Union army to flee from Manassas.

Procedures

- Preassign students to heterogeneous groups of four or five students.
- Present a list of approximately 10 to 15 key vocabulary terms to the students in a random order. Alphabetizing the list is one way to emphasize that students can use the words in any order.
- Have the groups use the words to predict a passage that could possibly reflect their use in the actual selection. If assistance is needed in understanding any of the given words, the teacher may want to discuss the unknown word or words in a meaningful context and draw out elaborations from the students. Or, students may choose to look up unknown words in the dictionary and select an appropriate definition.
- The groups can then read their predicted compositions to the remainder of the class, discussing the differences and similarities. During this portion of the procedure, students "exchange" their predicted passage by making comparisons and reacting to the selection from which the words were taken.
- One optional follow-up is to have students use the words in a passage that reflect the actual selection to reinforce their understanding of the content and the vocabulary.
- Another option is to have students finalize their compositions in either the predicting phase or the after reading phase by engaging in peer editing. Group members may elect or be assigned to such roles as researcher (if needed), content editor, contributing author, recorder, or proofreader. Figure 2 shows a sample exchange compare lesson on science while Figure 3 (p. 30) shows a sample lesson on political science. Figure 4 illustrates the Exchange Compare Strategy used in both the pre-reading and post-reading stages of a social studies lesson. Here, students, working in communal writing groups, review the key words/phrases and develop a composition reflecting the actual content of the material under study.

FIGURE 2
Sample Exchange Compare Lesson
Science: Ecology

I. **Key Concepts/Phrases:**

community	interactions
different	organisms
ecology	population
environment	scientist
habitat	species
individuals	tidepool

II. **Predicted Passage:**
Scientists have been observing individuals in their *habitats* and their *interactions* with other *organisms*. The *different species* share a *community* that forms the *ecology* of this particular *environment.* One particular *scientist* has been studying reasons why the *population* of hermit crabs has significantly decreased in the *tidepools* of the "low country" of South Carolina.

FIGURE 3
Sample Exchange Compare Lesson on Social Studies
Governments and Economic Systems

I. **Key Concepts/Phrases**

capitalism	production
communism	profit
competition	resources
economics	revolution
industry	socialism

II. **Predicted passage**

The *economics* of the United States is based on *capitalism*. Natural *resources* are used for the *production* of goods. Then these goods are sold for a *profit*. Anyone can start an *industry* or a business to sell things. Businesses are in *competition* with each other. Some countries have *communism* or *socialism*. In Russia there was a *revolution* to make communism the form of government.

FIGURE 4
Sample Exchange Compare Writing Lesson on Social Studies
The Ice Age

I. **Key Concepts/Phrases**

THE ICE AGE

600 million years ago	southward
glaciers and ice sheets	Arctic musk oxen
oceans	woolly mammoths
Great Lakes	died out
horse	change in climate
camel	moraines
elephant	New York

II. **Predicted passage**

The *Ice Age* started over *600 million years ago* when *glaciers* took over the *oceans.* There were no glaciers on the *Great Lakes* or in *New York*. *Arctic musk oxen* and *woolly mammoths died out* when the ice melted and caused a *change in climate*. They went *southward* to the *moraines*. Later, the *horse, camel*, and *elephant* appeared on the earth.

III. **Passage based on actual selection**

The earliest period in the earth's history when *glaciers* and *ice sheets* covered the earth began over *600 million years ago*. As the glaciers melted, low areas filled with water. That is how the *Great Lakes* and the *oceans* were formed. Some of the soil and rocks left behind formed ridges called *moraines.*

The modern *horse, camel* and *elephant* appeared during the *Ice Age.* When the ice melted, the animals went *southward. Arctic musk oxen* and *woolly mammoths* lived as far south as Michigan and *New York.* Some scientists think the *change in climate* caused some of these large mammals to die out. Others think they were killed by human beings.

Reprinted with permission of Karen D. Wood and Allyn and Bacon Publishing Co.
(From *Literacy Strategies Across the Subject Areas*, 2001)

STORY IMPRESSIONS

Story Impressions (McGinley & Denner, 1987) requires students to predict a story line using sequentially presented words or phrases derived from a selection to be read. Students then read the passage with their predictions in mind and then have the option of constructing another story line reflecting the actual content of the passage.

Procedures
- Pre-assign students to writing groups of four or five, and allow them to move their desks in a composing circle, if possible. Tell them that they will work together to predict a storyline based on some clue words they will be given.
- Discuss the importance of prediction to understanding by explaining that in order to predict and make reasonable guesses, readers must make use of all of their prior experiences on a topic. Utilizing their own background knowledge creates richer metal images and elaborations that, in turn, help them understand.
- Explain that it is often possible to make reasonable predictions about something with a minimal amount of information. Showing a portion of a familiar object or picture and having students guess the whole is one way to demonstrate this concept. Relate this to reading by telling students that previewing the title of a chapter, pictures, bold-face print, and subheadings beforehand helps readers develop a mental set for the content to be studied.
- Then, introduce key words and phrases on the board or an overhead or by giving each student or group a printed copy. Read through the words with the students and ask them to begin developing their impressions of what the story may be about. For modeling purposes you may want to "talk through" a short example initially with the class as a whole before breaking them into small groups.
- Tell the students that they will put their heads together to construct a single story. Remind them of their roles and functions within the group.
- Circulate around the groups to provide assistance wherever needed. If time is a problem, which is frequently the case in middle schools, a timer may be used to give the students a specified number of minutes to complete the task.
- Have the groups read their story impressions to the class and point out how varied, and yet equally acceptable, the responses can be. Pass out the original selection and have students read and make comparisons. The group concept can be continued here with students reading portions of the story and then retelling the information with group members.
- When making comparisons with the actual selection, assure students that closeness of match with the author's story is not that important. Afterwards, or the next day, the groups or the class as a whole use the key words to retell the events of the actual selection. Mention how powerful and potent key words can be in predicting and in helping to recall what has been read.
- Again another option is for students to use the key phrases and words, after reading, in a composition that reflects the actual events in the story. Figure 5 (p. 32) shows a sample story impressions lesson for language arts.

FIGURE 5
Sample Story Impressions Lesson for Language Arts
The Dinner Party by Mona Gardner

The words in the list below appear in this order in Gardner's story.

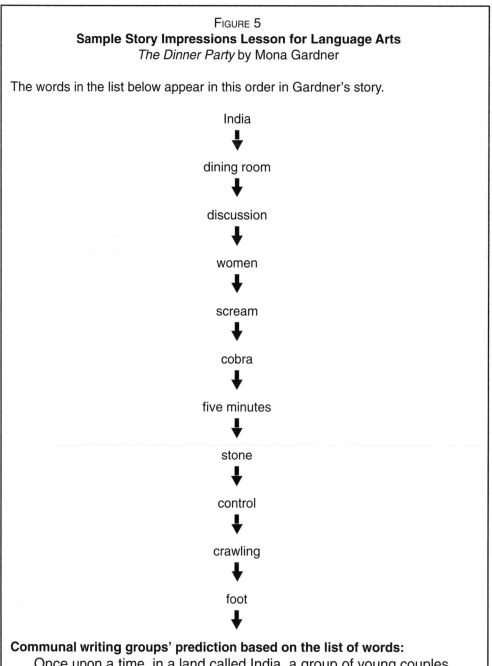

India
⬇
dining room
⬇
discussion
⬇
women
⬇
scream
⬇
cobra
⬇
five minutes
⬇
stone
⬇
control
⬇
crawling
⬇
foot
⬇

Communal writing groups' prediction based on the list of words:
Once upon a time, in a land called India, a group of young couples were eating in a dining room. They were having a pleasant discussion, when all of a sudden the women at the table screamed. There was a large cobra under the table, and it had been gnawing on someone's foot for five minutes without her knowledge. The woman who was bitten turned to stone, and everyone in the room was out of control crawling all over the floor to get away from her foot, where she had been bitten.

CAPSULE VOCABULARY

Capsule Vocabulary (Crist, 1975) is used in the *post-reading* stage, after reading the passage or studying the content as a means of reinforcing the learning of new terms and concepts. Both exchange compare writing and story impressions are used in the prereading stage with the option of use in the post-reading stage of an instructional lesson.

Procedures

- Select approximately 10 to 15 target vocabulary terms from a unit, chapter, or selection just studied to display and review. (Ideally these words would have already been introduced to the students in the pre-reading phase to enable them to focus on them while reading and learning).
- The teacher, with the aid of the class, reviews each term using it in a conversational context as much as possible. The teacher can model this process by using the term informally in conversational sentences to expand the meaning.
- The previous step helps students as they work in pairs to engage in a dialogue about the vocabulary terms. Pairs review the words in conversational sentences, checking off the terms as they are mentioned, used, and defined by partners. This helps them move beyond the rigid memorization tasks that typify vocabulary study and into a higher level of understanding and learning.
- In the next stage, students are pre-assigned to heterogeneous groups of four or five to use as many of the target words as possible in a composition. The teacher may want to time the partner dialogue step and the group composition process to expedite the procedure and help students stay focused. Figure 6 (p. 34) shows a sample capsule vocabulary lesson on science and Figure 7 (p. 35) illustrates the application to mathematics.

SUGGESTED ROLES FOR PEER EDITING

The teacher may decide to engage students in communal writing solely for the purpose of practicing writing and reinforcing concept knowledge. In that case, no formal editing would be required. However, another option is to have students finalize their compositions in either the predicting phase or the after reading phase by engaging in peer editing. The following are suggested roles for communal groups.

Contributor: All group members contribute ideas related to the topic
Recorder: Individual records the ideas suggested (in both rough and final draft stages)
Reader: Individual reads aloud the composition for the group to assess "soundness" (in both rough and final draft stages)

Proofreader: Group members (selected or all) proofread the composition for punctuation, grammar, content, spelling, etc.

Editor: Group-selected individual gives final stamp of approval to composition

---

FIGURE 6
Sample Capsule Vocabulary Lesson on Science
Arthropods

Step 1: Present vocabulary

arthropods	millipedes
exoskeleton	carnivorous
crustaceans	arachnids
gills	prey
segments	venom
centipedes	

Step 2: Review definitions

Teacher: *Animals with exoskeletons, such as crabs, do not have bones. Another name for exoskeleton is what, class?*

Students: *Armor, or a hard, rigid covering.*

Teacher: *In literature, we might use metaphorical or exaggerated language to say that the soldier displayed an exoskeleton of steel when interrogated by his captors. Describe the soldier's behavior and appearance.*

Step 3: In pairs, students engage in conversational dialogue

Student A: *I guess all arthropods have an armor called exoskeletons, don't they?*

Student B: *That's right, and jointed legs. And some, like crustaceans, breath through gills.*

Student A: *A turtle's shell is like an exoskeleton.*

Step 4: Partners work together to compose a paper on topic of arthropods

Arthropods are invertebrate animals that have *exoskeletons* and jointed legs. There are more kinds of arthropods than all other animal species put together. Some types of arthropods are *crustaceans, centipedes,* and *millipedes, arachnids,* and *insects.*

Crabs and lobsters are crustaceans. They breath through *gills* and their bodies are divided into *segments.* Centipedes and millipedes look like worms with legs. The difference between them is the number of legs on each segment. Also, centipedes are *carnivorous* and use poison to kill their food.

The name for arachnids came from a Greek myth about a woman named Arachne. Their bodies are divided into two main sections and they have eight legs. Spiders and scorpions are arachnids. They both kill their *prey* with *venom.* Ticks are also arachnids. They don't have venom, but they can spread diseases.

FIGURE 7
Sample Capsule Vocabulary Lesson on Mathematics
Metric Measures of Length

Step 1: Present vocabulary

meter	dekameter	centimeter
kilometer	decimeter	millimeter
hectometer		

Step 2: Review definitions with student input
Teacher: What does the prefix *kilo* tell us about the word *kilometer*?
Student A: *kilo* means 1,000.
Student B: *kilometer* must be a thousand meters.
Teacher: Suppose I said, "I'd walk a kilometer for a cold drink." Would I walk more or less than a mile?

Step 3: Students engage in conversational dialogue using vocabulary (in pairs)
Student A: Let's see, you'd measure the distance from my house to yours in kilometers.
Student B: And I guess you could measure the length of our driveway in dekameters.
Student A: ...or maybe meters since a meter is a little longer than a yard.

Step 4: Students compose a paper on topic (in pairs or small groups)
Measuring length using the metric system is easy if you know that the <u>meter</u> is the basic unit of length and everything is based on 10. Just be careful not to confuse <u>centimeter</u> and <u>hectometer</u> or <u>decimeter</u> and <u>dekameter</u>. Remember, a <u>millimeter</u> is not a million meters; it's 1/1000 of a meter. If you want to measure how tall you are, you'd use <u>centimeters</u>. A centimeter is 1/100 of a meter. If you wanted to measure the length of your street, you might use <u>dekameters</u>. A dekameter is 10 meters. <u>Kilometers</u> are used to measure long distances. In Europe they use kilometers instead of miles.

References

Calkins, L.M. (1994). *The art of teaching writing.* Portsmouth, NH: Heinemann.

Crist, B. (1975). One capsule a week: A painless remedy for vocabulary ills. *Journal of Reading, 19,* 147-49.

Donahue, P. L., Voelkl, K. E., Campbell, J. R., & Mazzeo, J. (1999). *NAEP 1998 reading report card for the nation and the states.* U.S. Department of Education, Washington, DC: Office of Educational Research and Improvement.

Manzo, A. V. (1975). Guided reading procedure. *Journal of Reading, 18,* 287-291.

Manzo, A. V., Manzo, U. C., & Estes, T. H. (2001). *Content area literacy: Interactive teaching for active learning* (3rd ed.). New York: John Wiley & Sons, Inc.

McGinley, W. J., & Denner, P. R. (1987). Story impressions: A pre-reading/writing activity. *Journal of Reading, 31,* 248-253.

Vacca, R. T., & Vacca, J. L. (1999). *Content area reading: Literacy and learning across the curriculum* (6th ed.). New York: Longman.

Wilkinson, L. C., & Silliman, E. R. (2000). Classroom language and literacy learning. In M.L. Kamil, P.B. Mosenthal, P.D. Pearson, & R. Barr (Eds.), *Handbook of reading research: Volume III* (pp. 337-360). Mahwah, NJ: Erlbaum.

Wood, K. D. (1986). How to smuggle writing into the classroom. *Middle School Journal, 17* (3), 5-6.

Wood, K. D. (1994). *Practical strategies for improving instruction.* Columbus, OH: National Middle School Association.

Using Oral Reading in Middle and High School Classrooms

Research/Theory/Rationale. Oral reading practices in the classroom have always presented a dilemma for teachers, especially at the middle and high school level where many students do not readily engage in silent reading of assigned texts. To address this issue, some teachers resort to round robin reading techniques where students take turns reading aloud, a practice *not* supported by research for any grade level (Tierney & Readence, 2000). Yet, oral reading can be an effective way to help students understand texts (Richards, 2000; Samuels, Schermer, & Reinking, 1992) because it leads to more fluent reading. Studies have documented a significant relationship between oral reading fluency and comprehension (Pinnell et al., 1995; Stayter & Allington, 1991; Zutell & Rasinski, 1991). Students can benefit from a gradual transition to more independent silent reading by participating in approaches that use oral reading in lively and enjoyable ways. The approaches described here (Wood, 1984; Wood & Algozzine, 1994) provide opportunities for middle and high school students, especially struggling readers, to develop fluency while interacting with the concepts being addressed.

PAIRED OR ASSISTED READING

The teacher methodically (or randomly) pairs two or more students together for the purpose of reading aloud in unison. Because the students are reading together, it lessens the likelihood that other students will clamor to correct the errors of their peers. The teacher may choose to read along to assist with the fluency if deemed necessary. Students find this approach satisfying because they have a partner to rely on and they rarely have to go it alone.

CLOZE PROCEDURE ORAL READING

For this approach the teacher reads a selection orally while the students follow along with their copy. At designated words or phrases the teacher pauses as the students "fill in the blank" with the missing words. This technique helps students maintain their places, causing them to attend to the page and make the speech-to-print match.

MUMBLE READING

The phenomenon of mumble reading (reading aloud softly, but under your breath) was observed and advocated by Cunningham (1978) when she witnessed her graduate students subvocalizing as they tried to make sense out of a strange alphabet. At selected points in a story, students may be told to mumble read to the end of the paragraph or page.

WHISPER READING

Although mumble reading is somewhat intelligible, whisper reading means carefully pronouncing the words but in a very soft voice. Students may be told to whisper read individually, with a partner or in a group.

CHORAL READING

When used judiciously, in combination with other methods, choral reading can be an enjoyable and engaging method to employ. Having students read in unison at a significant point in a selection can increase suspense or express an emotional reaction intended by the author.

IMITATIVE READING

Sometimes it is necessary to assist one or more struggling readers with their pacing and fluency. While pronouncing each and every word with precision is not necessary for comprehension, demonstrating an understanding of the prosodic cues of written language is essential. The teacher may choose to read a short section (usually dialogue) in an exaggerated tone and then call on one or more students to "repeat after me" in the same manner.

FOUR-WAY ORAL READING

In this approach, a combination of several methods can be used within the reading of a single lesson (Wood, 1984). For example, while reading a story from an anthology, the teacher may direct students to whisper read the first two paragraphs with a partner. Then they mumble read as a group to the end of the page. Choral reading may be used to express an important event, followed by assisted, imitative, and back to whisper reading. In these instances, the teacher leads the group in orchestral manner, maintaining a lively and interesting pace for the lesson.

PAIRED READING/RETELLING

Students can be paired to read silently or orally (using any of the methods described here) or in a combination approach. After designated segments (a page, a paragraph or two), they can take turns retelling the information in their own words. The partners should be told to elaborate, adding missing content, whenever necessary.

The classroom scenario in Figure 1 for Classroom A shows what occurs when Teacher X uses a traditional straight row, assigned seat approach and engages the class in round robin reading. The scenario depicted in Figure 2 for Classroom B shows what occurs when a collaborative model is used with students working in pairs, whisper reading, and engaging in a retelling of the assigned selection.

FIGURE 1
Classroom Scenario Using Round Robin Reading

Students in a social studies class are seated in straight rows and assigned seats. Each student is called on to read orally from the social studies textbook beginning with the first row. By the time the fourth student begins reading, the first three are gazing out the window, chatting with one another or passing notes. The next few students are busily reading ahead trying to rehearse their upcoming lines. A subsequent discussion of the story reveals that their comprehension and recall is sketchy.

FIGURE 2
Classroom Scenario Using Varied Approaches to Reading/Retelling

In another social studies class, students are asked to get into pairs and move their desks together. At times, partners take turns whisper reading paragraphs to each other. At other times, they read silently and take turns retelling the selection in their own words, elaborating on the content whenever necessary. When asked to engage in a group discussion after completing a few pages, all have had sufficient practice with the content and information to make the lesson successful and meaningful.

Shown in Figure 3 (p. 40) is an illustration of how some of the varied approaches to reading might be used in an actual classroom setting. The directives in *italics* indicate the teacher's instructions to the class.

FIGURE 3
Illustration of Multiple Approaches to Oral Reading/Retelling

Canada: A Varied Country
Chorally read the first paragraph.
Canada is the second largest country in the world. Only Russia is larger. In fact, Canada covers almost one half of the continent of North America. Unlike most countries of the world, Canada has oceans on three of its borders. The Atlantic Ocean is on the east, the Pacific Ocean is on the west, and the Arctic Ocean is on the north. Because of these ocean borders, Canada shares a land boundary in two locations with only one other country: the United States.

Question: How does the United States compare in size to Canada?

Whisper read the second paragraph with a partner.
Canada and the United States are friendly, and each nation likes and respects the other. Because they have such good relations, Canada and the United States share the longest undefended border in the world. Millions of Canadians and Americans cross the border every year. Sometimes, firefighters from the United States race across the border to help fight Canadian fires. Families from both countries often attend services in the same church or temple.

Question: What would the border with Canada be like if we were not friends?

Use paired reading with this paragraph.
Canada and the United States are alike in many ways. Both countries share many of the same major landforms, such as the Rocky Mountains. People in both countries speak English, although French is also an official language in Canada. And each nation is divided into smaller political units. We call ours *states*, and Canadians call their political divisions *provinces*. It is these similarities and close ties that make Canada a special neighbor.

Question: Retell in your own words what you learned in this paragraph.

Source: Hatfield, C. B., Kelly-Coupar, P., Hoh, C., & Lindsey, A. (1998). *World geography* (Grade 7). Parsippany, NJ: Silver Burdett Ginn, p. 73.

Some Final Notes
    A few important comments must be made to ensure successful incorporation of oral reading in the instructional lesson.

- Remember that the most important part of reading is comprehension – not pronouncing all the words correctly.
- Incorporate group retellings and questions requiring higher level thinking throughout the lesson to increase students' understanding of what is read.

- As the grade level and proficiency level of the students increase, decrease the amount of oral reading.
- For struggling readers, phase in paired or small group silent reading/retelling more frequently.
- Have students read a selection silently in preparation for the lively oral reading to follow.

References

Cunningham, P. M. (1978). Mumble reading for beginning readers. *The Reading Teacher, 31,* 409-411.

Pinnell, G. S., Pikulski, J. J., Wixon, K. K., Campbell, J. R., Gough, P. B., & Beatty, A. S. (1995). *Listening to children read aloud: Oral fluency.* Washington, DC: U. S. Department of Education, National Center of Education Statistics.

Richards, M. (2000). Be a good detective: Solve the case of oral reading fluency. *The Reading Teacher, 53,* (7), 534-39.

Samuels, S. J., Schermer, N., & Reinking, D. (1992). Reading fluency: Techniques for making decoding automatic. In S. J. Samuels & A. E. Farstrup (Eds.), *What research has to say about reading instruction* (2nd ed.) (pp.124-144). Newark, DE: International Reading Association.

Stayter, F. Z., & Allington, R. L. (1991). Fluency and the understanding of texts. *Theory into Practice, 30,* 143-148.

Tierney, R. J., & Readence, J. E. (2000). *Reading strategies and practices: A compendium.* (5th ed.). Boston: Allyn & Bacon.

Wood, K. D. (1984). Four-way oral reading: An alternative to round robin reading. *The Reading Teacher, 37,* 38-41.

Wood, K. D., & Algozzine, B. (1994). Using collaborative learning to meet the needs of high risk learners. In K. D. Wood & B. Algozzine (Eds.),*Teaching reading to high risk learners. An integrated approach* (pp. 315-333). Boston: Allyn & Bacon.

Zutell, J., & Rasinski, T. (1991). Training teachers to attend to their students' oral reading fluency. *Theory into Practice, 30,* 212-217.

Improving Students' Comprehension
by Developing Their Knowledge of Vocabulary

Research/Theory/Rationale. There is a strong relationship between knowledge of word meanings and reading comprehension (Anderson & Freebody, 1981; Davis, 1944; 1968; Thorndike, 1974). In fact, Davis (1944) went so far as to postulate that word knowledge is the most potent contributor to overall comprehension. More recent research also supports this view (Anderson & Nagy, 1993; Stahl, Hare, Sinatra, & Gregory, 1991; Hayes & Tierney, 1982). When teaching new vocabulary to students, it is important to consider three aspects of learning: (1) Students need to be actively engaged with the new information; (2) Learners must have multiple opportunities for exposure to the new terms; and (3) Instruction should always encourage independent learning. The vocabulary strategies described here meet each of these goals, and also provide teachers with the chance to gradually release the responsibility of learning to the student.

PREVIEW IN CONTEXT STRATEGY

The Preview in Context Strategy (Readence & Baldwin, 1981; Tierney, Readence & Dishner, 2000) is an expedient and beneficial way to pre-teach significant concepts from content area material. The technique combines a "definition approach" with a "context approach" to vocabulary learning, while dynamically engaging students with the new information, providing multiple exposures to the new terms, and encouraging independent learning.

Procedures
- Begin by selecting some important words from a passage, chapter, or segment of text. Choose words that are essential to the understanding of the selection, and limit the number of items to five or six key terms.
- Direct the students' attention to each word as it is used in the context of the selection. Read the sentence or sentences aloud to the class as they follow along in their text. Then, have them read the same sentence(s) silently.
- Begin a teacher-directed questioning strategy to help students use the context to derive meaning. To start the line of questioning, use questions such as, "What does the sentence tell you about the word?"

- Expand students' understanding of word meanings by helping them relate the word to other words (that is, connecting it to their schemata). Discuss similarities and differences to other words they know, discuss word parts, find synonyms and antonyms, or use the word in other contexts. Figure 1 is an example of the preview in context strategy applied to a social studies lesson.

FIGURE 1
Sample Social Studies Lesson
Teaching Vocabulary in Context

Farm Villages
    The farmers working these tiny fields are mostly subsistence farmers who grow food only for family use. They have little money to spend on modern farm machinery, insecticides, and fertilizer.

- Select significant vocabulary term, *"subsistence."*
- Orally read the word in context.
- Have students read silently.
- Ask students specific questions about what they think the word means. Another option is to encourage the use of visual/mental imagery here.

T: What do the surrounding sentences tell you about the word "subsistence?"
S: *I think it gives a negative view.*
T: What makes you think so?
S: *It says they grow food only for family use. Then it goes on to talk about how little money they have. Maybe it means poor.*
T: What are some other words you know with the prefix "sub?"
S: *subset (like in math), substandard, subterranean.*
T: What do you think that prefix means?
S: *Below, low, beneath.*
T: Is there another familiar word part in subsistence?
S: *-ist as in exist, which means to live.*
T: So, subsistence means what?
S: *To live below or beneath.*
T: Yes, the glossary says specifically subsistence means to remain alive (esp. on food) on a minimum livelihood.

VOCABULARY SELF-COLLECTION STRATEGY

The Vocabulary Self-Collection Strategy or VSS (Haggard, 1982, 1986) is another method of teaching and practicing the use of context to determine word meanings. It is a strategy in which student involvement is high, and it allows multiple exposures to words while fostering independent learning. Furthermore, it requires little preparation time for the teacher, and can be used either at the beginning of a lesson as a preview, or at the end of a lesson as a follow-up activity.

Procedures

- Tell the students to seek out one or more new and interesting words related to the unit of study. If possible, the words should be chosen from an environment outside of school. Field trips, videos, television, or any media print are good sources for new words.
- Students should begin to keep a personal notebook or vocabulary journal to document their words.
- The learners must include in their journal the context in which the word appeared. From there, they can try to deduce the meaning of the new word. (The "Preview in Context Strategy" described earlier is one effective way to model the use of context to determine word meanings.)
- Students should then select the dictionary definition that best supports the context in which the word is used. Again, modeling is important here, as students often tend to write down the first or shortest definition they can find. Be sure to emphasize *how* the word is used, including various parts of speech, when approaching this step in the procedure.
- To further expand word knowledge and understanding, allow the students the opportunity to record associations, such as structurally or semantically familiar words.
- Enhance student retention of the new word by instructing them to use the word (in its correct context!) in a sentence of their own construction.

Extend VSS to a Whole Class Activity

- When using this strategy in the classroom, have the students write their words on the board at the beginning of class. (or choose to divide the class into smaller groups, using some students' words one week and others' words the next).
- Ask each student to identify his or her word, its definition, where it was found, and why it is important to study.
- After all words are presented, the class should narrow the list to the most essential words.
- The originator of the word should again define it (with teacher assistance, if necessary), and the students can record the word in a "Class Words" section of their notebook.
- The reduced list (and any others the teacher may select) can be reviewed at the end of the week or unit of study.
- If desired, other assignments can be developed using the new words, such as writing with the words, making puzzles, or researching the etymology of the words.

PERSONAL VOCABULARY JOURNAL

Most of the vocabulary terms students learn are words chosen by the teacher – and often these terms are suggested by commercially prepared materials and textbooks. The Personal Vocabulary Journal (Wood, 1994, 2001) allows students to self-select their own vocabulary terms to develop at all grade levels and across all subject areas to help students' focus on new words in the classrooms or in their environments away from school. Figure 2 illustrates a page from a personal vocabulary journal.

Procedures

- Set the purposes for the journal by asking students if they have ever heard or read a word – in school or out – and wondered what it meant. Also, suggest the benefits of choosing their own vocabulary words to study instead of learning words as determined by the teacher.
- Show the students a blank "Vocabulary Journal" form – either as a handout or on the overhead. Tell the students that they will use this form to record one or two (or more) new words related to the current unit of study or that they find interesting.
- Demonstrate a sample entry by "thinking aloud" the means by which students would select and record a new word. Encourage class participation during this step wherever possible.
- Students can be assigned to small groups to share their choice of words from their vocabulary journals. When appropriate, they may be asked to "act out" their words or make a drawing showing its meaning.
- Also, students may be asked to select two to three words from their collection for weekly or unit quizzes. These terms can be submitted to the teacher for assessment purposes.

FIGURE 2
Personal Vocabulary Journal
English/Language Arts

My new word is <u>nemesis</u>

It is related to <u>a character in our English anthologies</u>

I found it <u>in a newspaper article and in our English book</u>

The specific context is <u>The first base player of the opposing team was Joe's worst nemesis</u>

I think it means <u>an enemy</u>

The appropriate dictionary definition is <u>an unbeatable rival</u>

It reminds me of <u>Batman and The Joker from my comic books.</u>

My sentence is <u>Lincoln Middle School is our basketball team's nemesis.</u>

GRAPHIC ORGANIZER

A Graphic Organizer is a visual aid that defines hierarchical relationships among concepts (Dunston, 1992; Moore & Readence, 1984). A Graphic Organizer can be used in any subject area to pre-teach and reinforce the technical vocabulary or to show how concepts/events/characters are related. Figure 3 (p. 47) illustrates a Graphic Organizer in science. The Graphic Organizer is most effective when used in the pre-reading stage of a lesson, during the reading to add additional information and contextual definitions, and in the post-reading stage to revisit, synthesize and review the new learning. More recent applications of the Graphic Organizer indicate increased benefits when teachers explain the relationships among the concepts, elicit student input, connect the new learning to previously learned information, continually refer to the text, and reinforce decoding and structural analysis when appropriate (Merkley & Jefferies, 2000/2001). Figure 4 (p. 48) shows a Graphic Organizer used throughout a lesson whereby students add to the clusters of information as they read.

Procedures
- **Concept identification.** Analyze the content to determine the most significant concepts.
- **Concept selection**. To avoid making the list overly complex, reduce the list to the most important concepts. Then classify the items in outline form.
- **Diagram construction.** Arrange the terms in a tree diagram that reflects the structure established in Step 2. Figure 3 (p. 47) illustrates how these terms can be arranged in a tree diagram on the animals with and without backbones. Figure 4 (p. 48) uses a graphic organizer to introduce key terms related to genetics. Whenever possible, use creativity in designing the graphic organizer. Figure 5 (p. 49) shows various band instruments. Figure 6 shows how a graphic organizer can be used to show concepts related to the early Greeks.
- **Initial evaluation.** Does the organizer accurately convey the concepts you wish to teach? Make sure it is not too complex since students can be overwhelmed if the visual display is too complicated.
- **Presentation of the organizer**. Visually display the organizer via handouts, a permanent poster, overhead transparency, or chalkboard.
- **Talk students through the organizer**. Explain each term, encourage student questions and discussion, and indicate the ways in which terms are related to each other. In so doing you will be developing vocabulary, improving reading comprehension, and enriching schemata in ways which will make subject matter more meaningful to students.
- **Encourage students to elaborate on the terms while reading**. Hand out copies of the guide before reading (or have students copy from your explanation). Then, ask them to add new facts, details and related information during their reading to further extend their understanding of new concepts and help solidify their understanding of key concepts.
- **Review the key concepts using the graphic organizer**. After reading, return to the graphic organizer and have the students discuss what they have now added from their reading and synthesize information from varied sources.

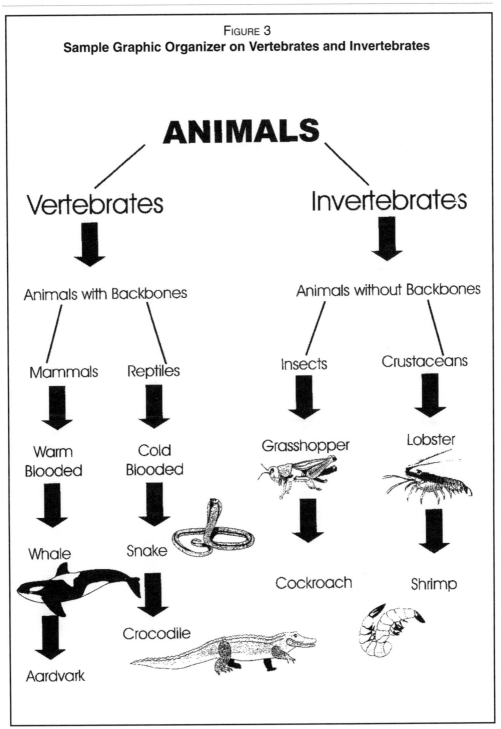

FIGURE 3
Sample Graphic Organizer on Vertebrates and Invertebrates

FIGURE 4
Sample Graphic Organizer with Student Notes on Science
Genetics: The Study of Heredity

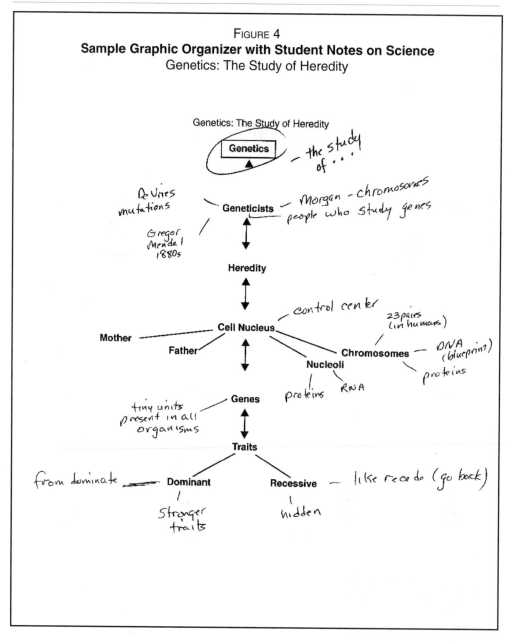

FIGURE 5
Sample Graphic Organizer on Music

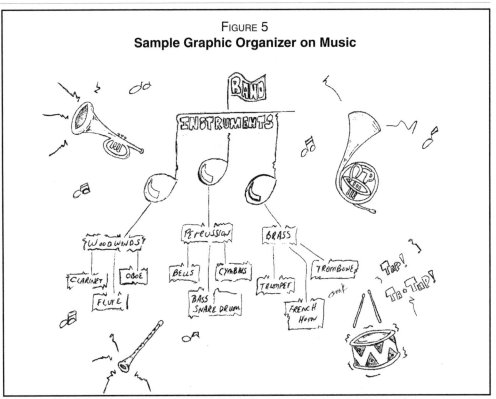

Thanks to Christopher Knight for contributing this example.

FIGURE 6
Sample Graphic Organizer
Social Studies

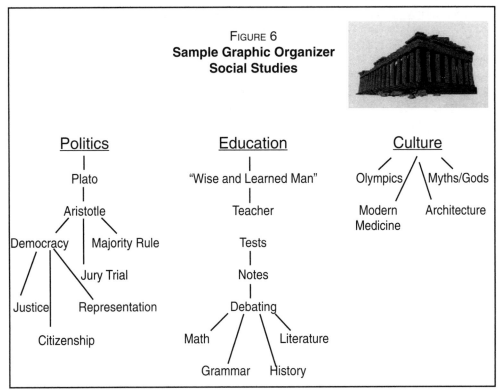

Thanks to teacher, Shelly Shope, for contributing this example.

References

Anderson, R. C., & Freebody, P. (1981). Vocabulary knowledge. In J. T. Guthrie (Ed.), *Comprehension and teaching:Rresearch reviews* (pp. 77-117). Newark, DE: International Reading Association.

Anderson, R. C., & Nagy, W. E. (1993). The vocabulary conundrum. *Technical Report No. 570.* ED 354 489.

Davis, F. (1944). Fundamental factors of comprehension in reading. *Psychometrika, 9,* 185-197.

Davis, F. (1968). Research in comprehension in reading. *Reading Research Quarterly, 3* (4), 499-545.

Dunston, P. J. (1992). A critique of graphic organizer research. *Reading Reseach and Instruction, 31* (2), 57-65. (ERIC Document Reproduction Service No. 441 050)

Haggard, M. (1982). The vocabulary self-collection strategy: An active approach to word learning. *Journal of Reading, 27,* 203-207.

Haggard, M. (1986). The vocabulary self-collection strategy: Using student interest and world knowledge to enhance vocabulary growth. *Journal of Reading, 29,* 634-642.

Hayes, D. A., & Tierney, R. J. (1982). Developing readers' knowledge through analogy. *Reading Research Quarterly, 17,* 203-207.

Merkley, D., & Jefferies, D. (2000/2001). Guidelines for implementing a graphic organizer. *The Reading Teacher, 54* (4), 350-357.

Moore, D. W., & Readence, J. E. (1984). A quantitative and qualitative review of graphic organizer research. *Journal of Educational Research, 78,* 11-17.

Readence, J. E., & Baldwin, R. S. (1981). *Content area reading : An integrated approach.* Dubuque, IA: Kendall/Hunt.

Stahl, S. A., Hare, V. C., Sinatra, R., & Gregory, J. F. (1991). Defining the role of prior knowledge and vocabulary in reading comprehension: The retiring of number 41. *Journal of Reading Behavior, 23* (4), 487-508.

Thorndike, R. L. (1974). Reading as reasoning. *Reading Research Quarterly, 9,* 135-147.

Tierney, R. J., Readence, J. E., & Dishner, E. K. (2000) *Reading strategies and practices:A compendium.* Boston: Allyn & Bacon.

Wood, K. D. (1994). *Practical strategies for improving instruction.* Columbus, OH: National Middle School Association.

Wood, K. D. (2001). *Literacy practices across the subject areas.* Boston: Allyn & Bacon.

6

Using Students' Background Knowledge
to Improve Vocabulary, Comprehension, and Writing

Research/Theory/Rationale. Descriptions of best practices in supporting reading always include the use of strategies for activating and building background knowledge (Hinson, 2000). The notion that we all possess a unique combination of experiences that can be used to aid in understanding is a prevalent one in the professional literature (Rumelhart, 1980; Spiro, 1977). "Schemata" is the name given to represent those abstract knowledge structures through which information and experiences are stored in our minds. Schema theory, then, is a theory about how knowledge is represented in memory. A schema-theoretic view of comprehension suggests that by stimulating readers' prior knowledge (e.g., getting them to talk about their experiences), their understanding of new information can be improved and their retention increased. Ample research supports this schema-theoretic view, some of which specifically demonstrates improved understanding when experiences are activated prior to reading a passage (Thames & Readence, 1988) and when experiences are enriched and elaborated after reading (Bean, Inabinette, & Ryan, 1983). The three teaching approaches described in this chapter, KWL Plus (Carr & Ogle, 1987; Ogle, 1986), Zooming In and Zooming Out (Harmon & Hedrick, 2000; 2001) and List-Group-Label and Write (Taba, 1967; Wood, 1986) highlight the use of students' experiences before, during, and after the reading of an assignment.

KWL PLUS

The KWL Plus strategy (Carr & Ogle, 1987; Ogle, 1986) supports reading comprehension in all subject areas through the use of brainstorming, purpose-setting, reflecting, and organizing information. It consists of four phases and promotes total class involvement. Figure 1 (p. 52) displays an example of a blank KWL form, and Figure 2 (p. 54) illustrates how KWL Plus can be applied to a secondary science lesson.

K—What I know
- Begin by asking students to brainstorm, that is, contribute anything that comes to their minds about a particular topic. The topic should be one about which students have at least some knowledge.
- Write the information on the board, a transparency, or individual worksheets in the format shown in the KWL Strategy Form.

FIGURE 1
KWL Strategy Blank Form
From Ogle (1986)

Name _____   Subject _____

Date _____

1. <u>K—What We Know</u>   <u>W—What We Want to Learn</u>   <u>L—What We Learned</u>
<u>and Still Need to Learn</u>

2. <u>Categories of Information We Expect to Use</u>
    A.   E.
    B.   F.
    C.   G.
    D.   H.

- To strengthen students' thinking abilities during the brainstorming activities, ask students to support selected answers by indicating where they learned the information or by explaining how they can substantiate their responses.
- For the next step in this phase, help students categorize the contributed information. This step gives structure to the class-generated associations and helps students think in categorical terms.
- Model the process of categorizing by initially providing examples through thinking aloud.
- Use this phase to assess the background knowledge of the students. If the background knowledge is insufficient, proceed no further with the lesson, and instead build their knowledge base through visual displays, demonstrations, and explanations.

W—What do I want to know?
- Ask students to determine what questions might be answered in the selection to be read. This may be done as a group activity or as an individual activity where each student writes personal questions on the strategy worksheets.
- To make this phase a more manageable task for the students, break the chapter or selection into topically-related sections to allow time for reflection and self-monitoring.

L—What I learned
- As students read, direct them to write any significant concepts they encounter on the "L" portion of their worksheet. These concepts may or may not have relevance to the questions originally posed.
- After reading, bring the class together to determine if the questions raised in the previous phase were adequately answered by the selection.
- Ask students to further elaborate on a question-response by adding newly learned information.
- Use the background knowledge displayed in the opening phase to help students understand and clarify the new concepts. For example, you might say, "The word *magma* was contributed in the first part of our lesson; what have you learned about that word now?"
- If questions are not addressed by the selection, ask students to seek further information from other sources.

Plus - The writing phase
- In this phase direct students to create semantic maps and to write a summary of the topic. Begin by modeling the map construction process as a class before assigning independent practice. Instruct students to use the KWL procedure to produce maps by categorizing the information listed in the "L" phase of the strategy. The resulting semantic map will include the main topic, categories about the topic, and supporting details for each category.
- Using their newly created semantic maps, instruct students to write a logical, comprehensible summary of the information.

ZOOMING IN AND ZOOMING OUT

Zooming In and Zooming Out (Harmon & Hedrick, 2000; 2001) is an instructional framework for assisting teachers in introducing and reinforcing the meaning of conceptually important terms in a specific content area. It also guides class discussions and readings about an important term that is critical for understanding the topic at hand. This framework is based upon the notion that concepts can be learned by closely examining specific features and traits (Zooming In) and by situating the concept within a larger picture (Zooming Out). For "zooming in," the teacher addresses important ideas about a concept and also provides non-examples about the concept. For "zooming out," the categories include an extension of similar concepts and also related ideas. There are five phases to this approach.

Phase l: Introduction
- Introduce the term or concept to be studied by writing it on a sheet of chart paper or a section of the chalkboard.
- Conduct a brainstorming session with the whole class by asking students to tell what they know about this term or concept.
- Write student responses on the chart paper. Students can copy these responses on their Information Sheet (see Figure 3, p. 55).

FIGURE 2
KWL Plus Sample Lesson for Science
Human Skeletal System

1. Whole Class/Small Group Contributions

K (Know)	W (Want to Know)	L (Learned)
Bones protect our organs Bones give our bodies shape and support Bones need calcium to stay strong Bones are hard and white	What are bones made of? How many bones are there? What is inside bones?	S-Bones are made of many tissues P-Bones are living organs L-There are 206 bones in your body of many sizes S-Bone marrow is soft tissue in many bones F-Blood cells are formed in red marrow P-Calcium and phosphorous make bones hard L-Bones are in all places of your body
Bones can be broken Bones have joints attached to them	How do broken bones heal? What kinds of joints are there?	S-There are immovable and movable joints P-Immovable joints don't allow much movement, but movable joints do L-Immovable joints are in places like your skull L-Movable joints are in many places, like your arm F-A fracture (broken bone) heals when new bone cells are made and cover the break and reshape the bone.

2. Class/Group Constructed Semantic Map

FUNCTIONS
Makes blood cells in red marrow
Heals fractures by making
  new cells and covering
  the break

Skeletal System

STRUCTURE
Bones are made of many tissues
Bone marrow is in many bones
Movable and immovable joints

PHYSICAL CHARACTERISTICS
Bones are living organs
Bones are hard and flexible because
  of calcium and phosphorous
Bones are many sizes
Joints hold bones together

LOCATION
206 bones throughout body
Immovable joints are in your skull
Movable joints are in your arm

(continued)

(Figure 2, continued)

3. Sample Summary for "Functions"

Our skeletal system does many things for our bodies. Our skeletal systems, mainly bones, protect our internal organs from being harmed. Bones also give our bodies support and structure. Bone marrow is inside our bones. Blood cells are created in the red marrow. When there is a fracture, bones make new cells, and cover the break; this is what allows our bones to heal.

FIGURE 3
Zooming In and Zooming Out
Information Sheet

Topic:
_____

Brainstorming notes:

Class notes from reading:

Zoom In Most Important:	Least Important:	Would not expect:

Zoom Out Similar to:	Related ideas:

Summary Statement

Phase 2: Text Interactions

- Select several texts for students to read about the topic. These may include textbook passages, encyclopedia references, readings from a website, or even an informational book from the library.
- Assign the texts to small groups of students to read.
- Tell each group to read about the topic and to take notes on the Information Sheet.
- After allowing enough time for this activity, bring the class together and compile students' findings on another sheet of chart paper labeled "Facts From the Readings."
- Have students reexamine the brainstorming sheet to decide if any information was incorrect. If so, draw a line through the incorrect information.

Phase 3: Zooming In

- Start this phase by explaining to students how some information is more important than other information. Tell students to examine both the brainstorming chart and the fact chart in their groups and to select three most important facts and three least important facts they want to remember about the topic. Model acceptable answers for the students.
- Once the student groups have their selections, allow students to vote on the three most important and three least important facts.
- Place this information on a third chart, entitled "Mapping." Have students copy this information on their own individual maps.
- Continue the whole class discussion by asking students to respond to non-examples. For example, one prompt could be "You would never expect Harriet Tubman to …"
- Write student responses on the mapping under the appropriate heading.

Phase 4: Zooming Out

- Continue the whole class discussion by asking students to think of ideas that are similar to the topic. Write these ideas on the map.
- Ask students to think of related ideas by using this prompt: "You cannot talk about _____ without talking about _____." Write these ideas on the map.

Phase 5: Summary Statement

- Once the map is completed, describe and model how to write a summary statement of the information on the map. See the examples of the map and summary statement illustrated in Figure 4 on the topic of "homesteading" as discussed in a history class. You can ask students to write a statement in ten words or less that captures the essence of the lesson. This activity may be done individually or in small groups.
- Ask students to share their summary statements.
- Have the class vote on the best summary statement.

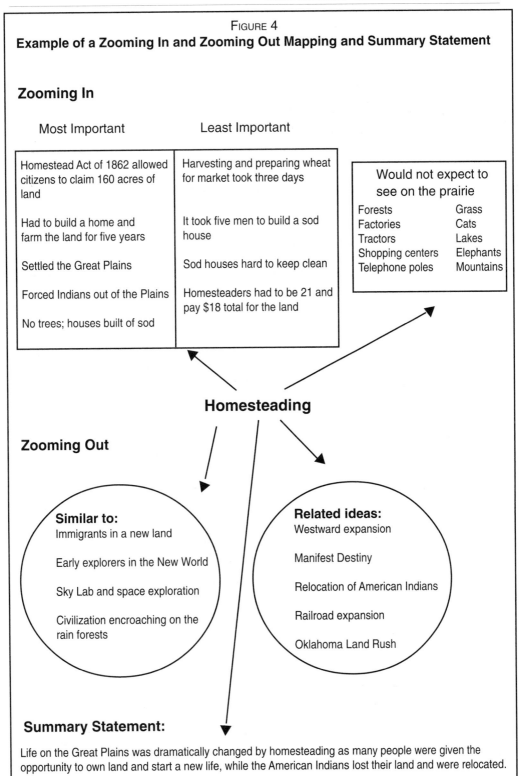

FIGURE 4
Example of a Zooming In and Zooming Out Mapping and Summary Statement

Zooming In

Most Important | Least Important

| Homestead Act of 1862 allowed citizens to claim 160 acres of land | Harvesting and preparing wheat for market took three days |

Had to build a home and farm the land for five years | It took five men to build a sod house

Settled the Great Plains | Sod houses hard to keep clean

Forced Indians out of the Plains | Homesteaders had to be 21 and pay $18 total for the land

No trees; houses built of sod

Would not expect to see on the prairie

Forests   Grass
Factories   Cats
Tractors   Lakes
Shopping centers   Elephants
Telephone poles   Mountains

Homesteading

Zooming Out

Similar to:
Immigrants in a new land

Early explorers in the New World

Sky Lab and space exploration

Civilization encroaching on the rain forests

Related ideas:
Westward expansion

Manifest Destiny

Relocation of American Indians

Railroad expansion

Oklahoma Land Rush

Summary Statement:

Life on the Great Plains was dramatically changed by homesteading as many people were given the opportunity to own land and start a new life, while the American Indians lost their land and were relocated.

Thanks to Jeannie Lehr for contributing this example.

List-Group-Label and Write

The ability to group and classify terms or concepts on the basis of their common elements is a higher order thinking skill. List-group-label and write (Taba, 1967; Wood, 1986; 2001) is a brainstorming strategy in which students recall as many terms as possible on a given topic and then group these terms according to their similarities. It can be used before and after the reading of a selection.

Procedures
- Tell the class to think of all that comes to their minds on the topic to be studied. This could be anything about which they have some prior knowledge. Then display these terms on the board or an overhead transparency. The teacher may choose to introduce (preteach) significant terms at this time as well.
- Either as a class or in small, heterogeneous groups, have students group the terms displayed. They may need to explain why they choose to put certain words/phrases in a particular category.
- After engaging the class in any other background building activities (e.g. watching a brief video clip, viewing pictures or demonstrations related to the topic), have the students read the selection.
- Tell the students to brainstorm about what they have learned on the topic after reading the selection, and display these associations as in step one. (Some of the terms mentioned previously may be repeated to validate what they knew before reading.)
- Again, have the students group and classify the terms displayed, justifying the categories if needed.
- Ask students to work in pairs or individually to choose a group of terms about which to write a brief paragraph. It may be necessary to model the composition of one or more paragraphs with the entire class before releasing the responsibility to the students. They can be encouraged to use the terms displayed and to refer to the selection whenever necessary.

Figure 5
Sample List-Group-Label and Write Exercise in Mathematics
Geometry

Sample Student Free Associations

point	circumstances	obtuse
line	semicircle	radius
diameter	center	compass
arc	vertex	ray
protractor	pi	sides
acute	right	endpoint
		ratio

(continued)

(Figure 5, continued)

Students Group and Label Terms
Terms about angles: vertex, sides, ray, endpoint
Types of angles: acute, right, obtuse
Devices for measurement: compass, protractor
Terms about circles: chord, arc, circumference, diameter, semicircle,
   radius, center, pi
Used in formula for pi: circumference, diameter, ratio
Units of length: point, line, endpoint, ray, line segment

Sample Paired Writing Exercise on One Category

Types of Angles

Angles are figures formed by two rays that have the same endpoints. The
endpoint is called the vertex. The rays are called the sides of the angle.

FIGURE 6
Sample List-Group-Label and Write Exercise in Science
Volcanoes

Sample student free associations BEFORE reading

lavas	erupt	caldera (opening)
hot	dormant	Mexico
magma	mountain	heat
ashes		

Students group and label terms

Places	Names	Types	Parts
Mexico	Mt. St. Helen	dormant	caldera
Hawaii	Krakatoa	active-erupt	ashes
Mountain	Vesuvius	extinct	lava

Student free associations AFTER reading

intermittent	volcanic bombs	Japan	magma chamber
gas	rock fragments	Italy	
melt	ten miles	cinders	

Students group and label these new terms

Beginning	Volcanic materials	Stages	Places
magma	lava	dormant	Hawaii
rock	rock fragments	active	Italy
melt	gas	extinct	Mexico
magma chamber	basketball	intermittent	Japan
ten miles			

Sample paired writing exercise on one category.

Types of Volcanic Materials
There are three types of volcanic materials that erupt from a volcano. Lava is
magma that comes out and blows down. Rock fragments can be large or small.
Some are as big as basketballs. Gas or steam also comes out of the caldera.

References

Bean, T. W., Inabinette, N. B., & Ryan, R. (1983). The effect of a categorization strategy on secondary students' retention of literary vocabulary. *Reading Psychology, 4,* 247-252.

Carr, E., & Ogle, D. M. (1987). K-W-L plus: A strategy for comprehension and summarization. *Journal of Reading, 30,* 626-631.

Harmon, J. M., & Hedrick, W. B. (2000). Zooming in and zooming out: Enhancing vocabulary and conceptual learning in social studies. *The Reading Teacher 54* (2), 155-159.

Harmon, J. M., & Hedrick, W. B. (2001). Zooming in and zooming out for better vocabulary learning. *Middle School Journal 32* (5), 22-29.

Hinson, B. (2000). *New directions in reading instruction (revised).* Newark, DE: International Reading Association.

Ogle, D. M. (1986). K-W-L: A teaching model that develops active reading of expository text. *The Reading Teacher, 39,* 564-570.

Rumelhart, D. E. (1980). Schemata: The building blocks of cognition. In R. J. Spiro, B. C. Bruce, & W. F. Brewer (Eds.), *Theoretical issues in reading comprehension* (pp. 33-58). Hillsdale, NJ: Erlbaum.

Spiro, R. J. (1977). Remembering information from text: The "State of Schema" approach. In R. C. Anderson, R. J. Spiro, & W. E. Montague (Eds.), *Schooling and the acquisition of knowledge.* Hillsdale, NJ: Erlbaum.

Taba, H. (1967) *Teachers' handbook for elementary social studies.* Reading, MA: Addison-Wesley.

Thames, D. G., & Readence, J. E. (1988). Effects of differential vocabulary instruction and lesson frameworks on reading comprehension of primary children. *Reading Research and Instruction, 27,* 1-12.

Wood, K. D. (1986). Smuggling writing into middle level classrooms. *Middle School Journal, 17,* 5-7.

Wood, K. D. (2001). *Literacy strategies across the subject areas: Process-oriented blackline masters for the K-12 classroom.* Boston: Allyn & Bacon.

Visual Imagery: Improving Students' Comprehension and Recall

Research/Theory/Rationale. Creating visual images during and after reading can have a positive effect on learning and recall (Gambrell & Bales, 1986; Peters & Levin, 1986; Pressley et al., 1995). This strategy enhances comprehension because it enables readers to use both verbal cues from print and image cues from memory to construct meaning while reading (Pressley, Woloshyn, & Associates, 1995). The tendency to engage in this process is differentiated across ability levels in that proficient readers spontaneously create and adapt visual images to draw conclusions, make interpretations, connect to personal experiences, and recall a text (Keene & Zimmermann, 1997). Struggling readers, on the other hand, tend to use visual imagery less often than their above average counterparts while reading both familiar and unfamiliar text material (Finch, 1982). However, studies indicate that instruction and training in using visual imagery while reading can help low average readers monitor their own comprehension more effectively and hence improve what they learn (Gambrell & Bales, 1986; Gambrell & Koskinen, 1982). This chapter describes a guided imagery lesson that is appropriate to use in any subject area.

GUIDED IMAGERY LESSON

The Guided Imagery Lesson (Wood, 1994) is an adaptation of the "mind's eye" strategy described by McNeil (1987) and a strategy for imaging developed by Mundell (1985). It is an appropriate technique for broadening students' conceptual understanding of subject matter material. It is easy to implement, appropriate in numerous circumstances, and motivating to even the most reluctant adolescent.

Procedures
- Help students develop their visualization skills by having them create visual images of familiar, concrete objects, such as a rose, a pier, or a frog. Tell the students to close their eyes and form a picture for these words by trying to sense how the object looks, sounds, feels, and smells. Discuss more of the varied images with the class, being certain to reinforce the personalized nature of the responses.
- Proceed from visual images of words to visual images of complete sentences by following the same procedure. For example, direct students to create images for sentences, such as: "A grandmother is cooking a turkey in the

kitchen." Before eliciting their responses, have students underline the words in the sentence that are needed to form a mental picture. (The likely choices in this sentence would be grandmother, turkey, and kitchen.) Ask students to describe their own kitchen or a relative's kitchen and elaborate on what else and why she may be preparing this meal.

- Move from personal sentences to more content specific sentences. Find sentences in the material students are reading in class.

Examples

"An amoeba will move slowly across a slide." (science)
"Custer told his men to stop on the hill before they reached the campsite." (history)

Have students select the words that aid in forming a mental picture.
Ask probing questions such as:
"What do you see in your mind?'
"Are there any prevalent smells?"
"What do you feel – emotionally or tactilely?"

- Before reading have students turn to a short selection or excerpt in the textbook or other classroom reading material. Tell them they are going to make "pictures" or a "movie" as they read through the passage. Instruct the class to select the key words in the title and try to describe everything that comes to their minds. Discuss the contributions made by the class.
- During reading assign the students to pairs and tell them to underline lightly in pencil or use a Post-It to flag the key words in the first topically relevant section often signaled by subheadings. After discussing their images with their partner, have students share their responses with the whole class. Proceed in this manner for a few more sections until the class seems to have a grasp on using imagery with longer discourse. Direct students to continue working in pairs, discussing their images, using probing questions, and even making graphic representations of the information if necessary.
- After reading, follow up with the class-wide discussion of the content, asking for elaborations and inferred details whenever appropriate. Extend the lesson by having students engage in a writing activity or assess what they have learned with an objective or subjective test.

Examples of Guided Imagery in Different Subject Matter Areas

Figures 1, 2, and 3 (pp. 63 and 64) show how guided imagery with teacher prompts can be applied across all subject areas including English/language arts, social studies, and science.

FIGURE 1
Excerpt from a Guided Imagery Lesson
Literature
Lost Chance

The old man was feeble. He could barely walk across the room to answer the door. His mouth dropped open when he saw his sister after all these years.

Teacher Probing Questions	**Student Responses**
1. Describe the old man and his environment – his dress, his surroundings.	Student A—He has strands of gray hair on his head. His mouth quivers as he talks and his hands shake.
	Student B—He is wearing a plaid, flannel shirt and wrinkled pants.
	Student C—He uses a cane to walk and sits in the same chair every day.
2. How do you envision his sister?	Student D—She is much younger although still an older woman.
	Student E—I think she's after whatever money he has.
	Student F—I think she's sincere. She's been searching for him for a long time and wants a family reunion.

FIGURE 2
Excerpt from a Guided Imagery Lesson
Social Studies
California Gold Fever

In 1849 many people moved to California any way they could. Word spread throughout the world that gold was found at John Sutter's mill. Many people made their money selling mining supplies to newcomers.

Teacher Probing Questions	**Student Responses**
1. What comes to your mind after reading the title?	Student A—I see people everywhere arguing, dealing, digging.
	Student B—I see a wagon train of people and wooden cars filled with shovels.
2. Tell how people got to Sutter's Mill.	Student C—Some rode on horseback.
	Student D—Boats, wagons.
	Student E—On foot, in carriages.

(continued)

(Figure 2, continued)

3. How were they dressed?

Student F—The women wore bonnets and long dresses; the men wore boots, chaps, and heavy shirts.

Student G—Their clothes were dirty and dusty and because they could not get cleaned regularly.

4. Describe the scene you see when mining supplies are being sold.

Student H—I see a store with a wooden floor and shelves filled with picks, shovels, and tin pans.

Student I—I see men arguing over the high prices.

Student J—One miner has a beard and appears tired but eager; the other one, the storekeeper, wears an off-white shirt with a black band on his upper hand.

FIGURE 3
Excerpt from a Guided Imagery Lesson
Science
Earthquakes

In addition to the violent movements of the earth's surface, earthquakes can cause huge sea waves that devastate the land. These waves, called by the Japanese name "tsunami," often occur in the Pacific Ocean where there is greater prevalence of earthquakes.

Teacher Probing Questions

1. Describe what you see happening around you as an earthquake begins to occur.

2. Your home near the ocean is threatened by a tsunami. Tell what you see.

Student Responses

Student A—The Weaver Building in the center of town begins to quiver and is the first to fall.

Student B—People are running, screaming, covering their children.

Student C—An alarm sounds and everyone heads for the basement of the school.

Student D—A huge, overpowering, dark blue and white wave is above me. I scream and run.

Student E—The land is drowning in water. People drift by in floats or on pieces of wood.

Student F—The entire atmosphere is darker. Whole houses are under water. People try desperately to get to dry land—running, swimming, clinging to their belongings.

IMAGINE, ELABORATE, PREDICT, AND CONFIRM (IEPC)

IEPC is a strategy to help students increase their understanding and recall by using visual imagery to predict events in a selection (Wood, 2001). It begins with the teacher modeling how to imagine a scene, adding details to this mental scene, and then predicting a possible story line. After reading, students confirm or disconfirm their original predictions. The specific components of IEPC are

Imagine: Close your eyes and try to imagine the scene. Share your thinking with a partner and the whole class.

Elaborate: Think of details surrounding the scene in your head. How do you think the characters feel? What are similar experiences? Describe the scene. What do you see, feel, hear, smell?

Predict: Use what you have imagined in your head to predict what might happen in the story (characters, events, setting, etc.).

Confirm: During and after reading the selection, think about your original predictions. Were they true, false, or were they not explained in the passage? Modify your predictions to coordinate with the actual selection.

Procedures
- Decide upon an appropriate tradebook, basal selection, or passage with content appropriate for developing imagery.
- Display the IEPC blank form on the overhead projector and tell the students that they are going to engage in a strategy designed to encourage them to use their imaginations to create pictures of what they see in their minds. Tell them that making pictures or images before, during, and after reading will help them understand and remember what they read.
- Use the transparency to point out and explain the four phases of IEPC using language appropriate to students' ability levels.
- Tell the students that they are going to read/hear a selection. Begin with the imagine phase and ask the students to join you in closing their eyes and imagining everything they can about the selection to be read. This may be based upon the cover of a book, a title, or a topic. Encourage the students to use sensory experiences by imagining feelings, taste, smell, sight, and surroundings.
- Talk aloud your thinking and then ask the class if they have anything to add. Write the responses in the "I" column on the form.
- Model for the students how to use their visual images and add details, anecdotes, prior experiences, sensory information, etc. and jot this information in the "E" column.
- Talk aloud at least one sample prediction, based upon prior visual images and encourage the students to do the same. Write these responses in the "P" column.
- Have the students read/listen to the selection (or segment) with these predictions in mind.
- After reading, return to the transparency and, using a different color marker, modify the original predictions to coordination with the newly learned information. Figure 4 (p. 66) shows how IEPC was used with an informative article from the magazine, *Time for Kids*, on the topic of mummies.

Figure 4
Sample IEPC Lesson for Social Studies
Time for Kids
"Valley of the Mummies"

Imagine	Elaborate	Predict	Confirm
– dark caskets	– casket shaking, hand poking out	– Egypt has mummies in pyramid	– No, mummies buried in tombs
– people under a pyramid looking	– busted out of the casket	– skin & bones found on mummi-fying table, body in a spiked coffin	– No, they found the bodies lying on cut stone
– sarcophagous	– eyes hanging out of head		– No hieroglyphics, decorations
– man making coffin	– screw up nose, pull out brains	– find coffin with hieroglyphics on it	– No, mummy had cancer
– movie of the mummy	– people came out of tombs, touched wraps, turned into mummies	– mummies without tongues	– Yes, poison powder
– archaeologist and a family		– dig bodies, booby traps come to hurt them	– No scrolls, bracelets, charms, and gold masks
– jewelry	– people showing everyone the hieroglyphics, it's a secret code	– digging up tombs, secret scrolls	– found governor of one of the lands
– men digging up		– find jewelry	
– tomb under ground	– mummies came alive because we read something we weren't supposed to		
– mummifying			
– bodies taking hearts	– ancient scroll, head had the Pharaoh golden face		
– digging in traps			
– taking jewelry			
– hieroglyphics			

A special thanks to teacher, Shelly Shope, for contributing this lesson.

FIGURE 5
Sample IEPC Lesson for English/Language Arts
Greyling by Jane Yolen

Imagine	Elaborate	Predict	Confirm
– I smell fish	– The couple was talking about having a child and the woman started to cry	– I predict the couple will have a baby and be happy forever.	– The husband found a seal, carried it home, and when the wife checked inside the shirt, it was really a baby boy.
– I hear a couple talking to each other	– A man went to catch fish in a pond and you could smell the fish after he caught it	– I think the couple will have a baby, and the father will get a fishing job and buy a real house to live in.	– The baby had silver eyes and hair and the couple named it Greyling.
– I see a shack			
– I see people hugging each other			
– I hear the ocean rolling into shore	– The man has one room in the hut filled with all his fishing gear. That room smells like fish	– Is this story fiction? Then I think the couple will have a baby that is half human and half fish.	– They got a new little hut still covered in moss by the sea. The fisherman did not get a new job.
– I see the forest with snow on top of the trees			
– I smell pine	– There is an old shack that has rotting wood and is covered in moss. There are pieces of cloth that cover the windows and the wind is blowing them open.	– I think the couple will adopt a child and the father will start setting up a fishing business which will bring in more money for the child to live happily.	– The man found a selchie which is half human, half seal. He went into the water to save the fisherman.
– I see sand			
– I feel seashells in my hands			
– I feel sand between my toes			
– The sun is blazing on my face			
– I hear birds squawking	– People are hugging each other because they are sad about not having children and are trying to comfort each other	– I predict the couple won't have a child because they want it to be around people and the live alone at the beach.	– When the selchie entered the water he turned into a seal again and seemed very happy about it.
– I hear the wind ringing in my ears			
– I feel the cool wind brush across my hot cheeks			
– I feel rocks beneath my feet	– There are pine trees in the forest and people are walking through the forest smelling the scent of pine	– I think the fisherman will catch a seal while he is fishing and the seal will grant him three wishes. One wish will be to have a child. His wife will be so happy but something will happen to the child later in the story.	– The boy longed to go to the ocean but was never allowed to enter water so when he got the chance to save his father, he willingly took it.
– I hear a seal crying			
– I see something flying out of the water			
– I see one lonely hut sitting on the beach	– People are walking on the beach—they feel the sand in their toes and the rocks are cutting the bottoms of their feet		– The couple did have a child but then had to give it back to the sea.
– I see a small room filled with fishing gear			
– I hear a woman crying			– There was a big storm and the fisherman was caught in it. No one would save him. Fisherman's wife wouldn't let her son help.
– I taste salty ocean water	– The couple is looking into a pond for fish. They see a mother fish having babies which upsets the woman in the story.		

A special thanks to teacher, Clare Endres, for contributing this lesson.

References

Finch, C. M. (1982). *Fifth-grade below average and above average readers' use of mental imagery in reading familiar and unfamiliar text.* Paper presented at the National Reading Conference, Clearwater Beach, FL. (ERIC Document Reproduction Service No. LD228-634)

Gambrell, L. B., & Koskinen, P. S. (1982). *Mental imagery and the reading comprehension of below average readers: Situational variables and sex differences.* Paper presented at the annual meeting of the American Educational Research Association. New York.

Gambrell, L. B., & Bales, R. J. (1986). Mental imagery and the comprehension-monitoring performance of fourth and fifth grade poor readers. *Reading Research Quarterly, 21* (4), 454-464.

Keene, E. O., & Zimmermann, S. (1997). *Mosaic of thought: Teaching comprehension in a reader's workshop.* Portsmouth, NH: Heinemann.

McNeil, J.D. (1987). *Reading comprehension: New directions for classroom practice* (2nd ed.). Glenview, IL: Scott, Foresman and Company.

Mundell, D. (1985). *Mental imagery: Do you see what I say?* Oklahoma City, OK: Oklahoma Sate Department of Education.

Peters, E.E., & Levin, J.R. (1986). Effects of a mnemonic imagery strategy on good and poor readers' prose recall. *Reading Research Quarterly, 21,* 161-178.

Pressley, M., Woloshyn, V., Burkell, J., Cariglia-Bull, T., Lysynchuk, L., McGoldrick, J., Schneider, B., Snyder, B. L., & Symons, S. (1995). *Cognitive strategy instruction that really improves children's academic performance* (2nd ed.). Cambridge, MA: Brookline Books.

Wood, K. D. (1994). *Practical strategies for improving instruction.* Columbus, OH: National Middle School Association.

Wood, K D. (2001). *Literacy strategies across the subject areas: Process-oriented blackline masters for the K-12 classroom.* Boston, MA: Allyn and Bacon.

Using Writing Frames to Help Students Construct Meaning

Research/Theory/Rationale. There is ample evidence in existing research that writing is an important venue for supporting learning across the curriculum (Dahl & Farnan, 1998). While writing tasks should aim toward reflection and elaboration of ideas, for struggling readers such tasks may prove to be overwhelming. Frequently, these students have great difficulty getting started and keeping focused on an issue when asked to respond in writing to a selection they have read. One teaching technique, called writing frames, is designed to meet the needs of these struggling learners (Fowler, 1982; Nichols, 1980). Writing frames are structures containing key language information to help students write about the major ideas of either a narrative or an expository passage. These frames contain connectives (i.e., *next, finally, then*) which aid in the transition from one idea to another, thus giving students a framework for developing a logical, coherent piece of writing. As evident in the examples provided in Figures 1 through 5, writing frames are appropriate for any content area, including mathematics. These frames can even be used to help students write about field trips (see Figure 6, p. 72) they have experienced (Wood, 2001).

PARAGRAPH FRAMES

Procedures

- Begin by explaining the process of the lesson to the entire class. The purpose in this instance would be to help students organize their thoughts into a logical, written form.
- Display the frame before reading (or listening) to the story or passage. This can be accomplished via an overhead projector or the blackboard.
- Tell the students to read (or listen) to a sample selection with the framework in mind. The frame then provides them with a purpose for reading (or listening).
- Help students fill in each line of the frame. Be prepared to narrow the focus of their responses since initially they may be inclined to trail off into an abundance of unnecessary details. Also, although numerous responses may be possible, encourage the students to reach a consensus on the information to be included.
- Allow student volunteers to read the completed writing frame orally. Have them evaluate the finished product to determine if it adequately reflects the events in the selection and if it requires additional revision stylistically.

- Assign a selection (preferably from the students' textbooks) to be read either silently or orally. (Reading orally can be done in pairs at low volume.)
- Permit students to work in pairs or groups to produce one common frame.
- Direct students to take turns reading and editing their completed frames. After the final editing, have students turn in the finished product for credit and/or class displays.
- Assign the frames as an independent activity after modeling and practicing various frames, and also when the students seem to understand the concept. Various frames can be reproduced and placed in an easily accessible area in the classroom. Students can read selections (either assigned or self-selected) and fill in the appropriate frame. These completed frames must be shared and edited by a partner before being turned in for credit.

Figure 1
Character Analysis Frame
Character Analysis
(Nichols, 1980)

In the story _____ by _____
the major character is _____, who is _____.
Another main character is _____. The problem
the major character has is _____
_____.
The story ends with _____. The lesson I
learned from reading this story was that _____
_____.

Figure 2
Essay: Time Order Frame
Essay: *Time Order*
(Nichols, 1980)

At the end of _____ what happened was that _____
_____. Previous to this
_____. Before this _____
_____. The entire chain of events
had begun for a number of reasons including _____
_____. Some prominent incidents
which helped to trigger the conflict were_____
_____
_____.

FIGURE 3
Essay: Comparison-Contrast Frame
Comparison—Contrast
(Nichols, 1980)

_____ are different from _____in several ways. First of all, _____, while _____ _____. In addition, _____ _____, while _____ _____. So it should be evident that _____ _____.

FIGURE 4
Sample Important Idea or Plot Frame for English/Language Arts
English/Language Arts
Important Idea or Plot

In this story the problem starts when Paul heard the sound of footsteps while "housesitting" in Mrs. Harland's old, creaky home. **After that**, he saw something at the end of the hallway that was tall and white. **Next**, he became even more frightened when he found a note warning him to "Leave this house." **The problem is finally solved when** the police called saying they just found three young thieves leaving the basement window of the house. **The story ends** with Paul lying in bed laughing to himself as he suddenly hears the sound of footsteps once again.

FIGURE 5
Sample Frame for Mathematics
Mathematics
Word Problem

Word Problem: Jack spent $9.99 for a movie video and bought 3 CDs for $15.98 each. He gave the salesperson $70.00 in cash. How much change should he get back if the sales tax was $4.35?

Writing Frame: To solve this problem, **first** multiply $15.98 by 3 to get the total cost of the CDs. **Second,** add the cost of the CDs to $9.99 to get the cost of both the CDs and the movie video. **Then,** add that amount to the sales tax of $4.35. **Finally,** take this total amount and subtract it from $70.00. What is left is the change the salesperson should give to Jack.

FIELD TRIP WRITING FRAME

The Field Trip Writing Frame (Wood, 2001), like the story frame format described previously, is a sequence of spaces connected by key language elements to help students focus their writing. This frame also enables teachers to "smuggle" writing into field trips in a non-threatening, enjoyable manner. The frame itself can be modified to include language elements that reflect the major topics under study.

Procedures
- Display the blank form on an overhead projector and explain to the class that this frame is designed to help them summarize important experiences on the field trip they are about to take. NOTE: Teachers may find it helpful, but not always necessary, to introduce the field trip writing frame after modeling and practice of story frames.
- In order to model and demonstrate its use, the teacher and students may take a brief tour of the school or surroundings, with the frame elements in mind. Then together they can fill in the frame by noting what was observed or experienced. The teacher may choose to "think aloud" the first few sentences.
- Before going on the actual field trip, remind the class that they will be summarizing the event by describing their experiences on the writing frame. Students can be assigned a partner, particularly if extra support is needed, or they can work alone to produce their recollection of what occurred on the trip and what they learned in the process.
- Students may be asked to illustrate their frames to coordinate with what was observed on the trip.
- Have students proofread their frames with a partner or small group.
- Students may be asked to volunteer to read their frames orally to partners or the class.
- Display the completed frames and illustrations in the classroom.

FIGURE 6
Sample Field Trip Frame

Name _Demarcus_   Partner _Keosha_

Yesterday I went to _Discovery Place_ with my class. The first thing I saw _was the rainforest room._ Next, _we saw an optical illusion wheel._ Then, _we saw an exhibit about the planets and how far away they are_. After that _we saw a huge model of a human eyeball_. Then _we got to make a cool picture using a pendulum and a marker_. I also learned _that static electricity can make my hair stand straight up_. If we go back again, I _would want to see a movie in the Omnimax Theater_.

References

Dahl, K. L., & Farnan, N. (1998). *Children's writing: Perspectives from research.* Newark, DE: International Reading Association.

Fowler, G. L. (1982). Developing comprehension skills in primary students through the use of story frames. *The Reading Teacher, 36,* 176-179.

Nichols, J. N. (1980). Using paragraph frames to help remedial high school students with writing assignments. *Journal of Reading, 24,* 228-231.

Wood, K. D. (2001). *Literacy strategies across the subject areas: Process-oriented blackline masters for the K-12 classroom.* Boston: Allyn & Bacon.

Verbal Rehearsal: The Value of Retelling for Improving Comprehension and Recall

Research/Theory/Rationale. Showing students how to put information in their own words, called retelling, self-recitation, or verbal rehearsal, is a powerful technique for enhancing comprehension (Searfoss, Readence, & Mallette, 2001). Students can engage in retelling in three ways: 1) orally, talking aloud to themselves or to another person; 2) graphically, writing down information in their own words; and 3) mentally, reviewing content in their heads. Regardless of mode (oral, graphic, or mental), students are actually summarizing what they have read. Empirical research supports the use of summarization to improve recall, retention, and comprehension (Devine, 1991; Palinscar & Brown, 1983; Taylor, 1992). Furthermore, reviews of research also indicate that summarizing information is only effective if it has been thoroughly modeled and demonstrated (Anderson & Armbruster, 1984; Devine, 1991; Hill, 1991). In this chapter we provide several approaches for teaching students how to summarize both orally and graphically.

MODELING THE PROCESS OF RETELLING

Koskinen, Gambrell, Kapinus, and Heathington (1988) have suggested a model for teaching students how to put information in their own words. The following sequence (Wood, 1994) is adapted from their recommendations.

Modeling the process
- *Explain the purpose and rationale.* Ask students if they have ever had any difficulty remembering what they read or hear. Explain how reciting the content in their own words can help them. Use everyday examples about telling a friend about a new movie or a trip they have taken.
- *Model and demonstrate.* Read aloud a brief passage of approximately 50 to 100 words from a textbook selection. Then retell the content in two or three sentences. Share your thinking orally in order to make the process more concrete and understandable. A sample dialogue might be: "As I read the selection to you about making silk, listen for the important ideas. Then, I will retell the passage using my own words."
- *Sample passage:*
    Making silk: Silk comes from silkworms which hatch from the eggs of a large white moth. They eat a great many mulberry leaves daily. After a month or so, the worms are fully grown. They begin to make themselves

a covering, called a cocoon. Many caterpillars do the same thing, but the cocoons of silkworms are made of a long silk thread. The cocoons are then sold to silk factories. People in factories work with millions of cocoons to turn them into silk threads, then into cloth. Silk cloth is very beautiful. What makes it so costly is the long time and great care that go into making it.

Teacher: Now I will retell the passage without looking back to the text. Silkworms hatch from moth eggs and begin to eat mulberry leaves every day. In a month, they grow and make a cocoon of silk thread that is sold to silk factories. There, the silk threads are turned into expensive cloth.

Teacher: How did I do? Did I include the main points?

The students may contribute other ideas at this point.

Guided Practice
- Provide another passage on the overhead projector and ask the class as a whole to retell the content.
- Write the class-generated retelling on a transparency.
- Next, group students in four or fives (or pairs) to engage in communal writing of a selection retelling.
- If additional practice is deemed necessary, assign students to work in pairs to practice the summarizing/retelling process.

Independent Practice
- Instruct students to write their retellings individually as they read portions of the textbook.
- This is similar to the hierarchical summary described next.

Transfer and Application
- Make students aware that retelling can aid them in understanding and remembering material both in and out of school.
- Tell students that they can engage in silent verbal rehearsal, retelling information in their head (rather than writing it down) whenever they want to ensure retention.

Hierarchical Summary Writing

Taylor (1992) has used what she terms hierarchical summaries with much success. In this technique students summarize in writing the most important ideas from a textbook selection.

Procedures
- Direct students to read the first section of the text and to write the most important ideas about the topic. Figure 1 illustrates this approach with a health lesson.
- Tell students to continue this process for subsequent sections and to limit their summaries to two or three sentences, if possible.
- Use the model for retelling described previously to prepare students for this procedure.
- After summarizing the assigned selection, tell students to review what they have written, reciting the content in their own words. In this way, the actual textbook headings alone can provide the stimulus for review.

Figure 1
An Example of a Hierarchical Summary for Health
Topic: Health
Chapter 7: Protecting Yourself Against Communicable Diseases

Microorganisms in Your World

We're never alone. Millions of microorganisms, microscopic living creatures, are everywhere. Most are harmless.

Two Kinds of Disease

Communicable diseases are caused by microorganisms and can pass from one person to another. They usually happen quickly. Noncommunicable diseases are not caused by microoogranisms, are not passed from person to person, and usually come from unhealthy living. They usually form slowly.

Microorganisms in Trash and Garbage

Microorganisms need food, water, and a warm, dark place to multiply. That's why they are often in trash and garbage cans.

SEQUENTIAL SUMMARY WRITING

The Sequential Summary Writing approach is based on the use of time order sequences typically found in narrative texts. Applying time order sequence, or narrative chronology, to expository material can help students with summary writing, because students are familiar with narrative organization (Hill, 1991; Pincus, Geller, & Stover, 1986; Taylor, 1992).

Procedures
- Begin by having students examine the selected passage to find major events.
- Ask students to decide if the major events occurred in a particular order.

- Have students then complete a Sequential Summary Frame (see the example in Figure 2) where they write the events in chronological order.
- Proceed to more abstract summary writing, such as cause-effect, compare-contrast, or problem solving, with frames that highlight these text patterns.

FIGURE 2
Sample Sequential Summary Frame for Social Studies
Selection: "The Growth of European Empires"

First, this happened: *Industrialization caused countries to expand overseas. They needed raw materials and markets for selling the goods.*

Then, *European governments took control of various countries' political and economic life. This way of expanding industry and trade is called "imperialism."*

Finally, *by the 1900s, many countries were colonies of the industrialized nations.*

MAGNET SUMMARIES

Buehl (1995) advocates the use of Magnet Summaries to help students organize important information into summaries. This approach is based upon the use of key words or concepts (magnet words) as concrete structures for guiding summarization.

Procedures
- Direct students to read a passage to find three or four key words or concepts (magnet words) that represent what the author is describing.
- Model the process by writing the magnet words on the chalkboard or overheard projector and then asking students to provide details that support the first magnet word. Write these words or phrases around the magnet word.
- Tell the students that they will write this information on an index card. Direct them to work cooperatively in groups to select remaining magnet words to complete in similar fashion, each on a separate index card.
- Once all groups have completed the index cards, model for the students how to take the information from one card to write a summary statement.
- Have the students work in their groups to write summary statements for the remaining magnet words, underlining the magnet word in each statement. Indicate to students that they do not have to use all the details they included on each card.
- Direct students to arrange their summary statements into a summary paragraph. They may have to change sentences around and add connective words to make the paragraph flow. Have students read their summary paragraphs aloud to determine if it sounds right. See the sample summary on "The Great Depression" for American history displayed in Figure 3 (p. 77) and one on "Literature" for a Spanish class displayed in Figure 4 (p. 78).

FIGURE 3
Sample Magnet Summary for History
Subject: American History
Topic: The Great Depression

Words	Summary Statements
changing lifestyles popular sports motion pictures **Roaring Twenties** people spending money more consumer goods	During the **Roaring Twenties,** Americans were enjoying new lifestyles that included spending money on pleasures, such as sports and motion pictures, and on readily available consumer goods.
1929 stock market crash Great Depression failed businesses **Hard Times** closed banks family fortunes lost no work widespread hunger	In 1929 **hard times** began when the stock market crashed, causing banks to close, businesses to fail, families to lose their fortunes, and ultimately, widespread hunger and unemployment.
1932 Franklin Roosevelt help from the government **New Deal** relief recovery reform WPA TVA Social Security Act	In 1932, President Roosevelt designed a government program, called the **New Deal**, to provide relief, recovery, and reform to help the American people get on their feet.

Summary Paragraph

During the **Roaring Twenties**, Americans were enjoying new lifestyles that included spending money on pleasures, such as sports and motion pictures, and on readily available consumer goods. Unfortunately, **hard times** began in 1929 when the stock market crashed, causing banks to close, businesses to fail, families to lose their fortunes, and ultimately, widespread hunger and unemployment. To solve this problem, President Roosevelt designed a government program in 1932, called the **New Deal**, to provide relief, recovery, and reform to help Americans get back on their feet.

FIGURE 4
Sample Magnet Summary for Foreign Language
Subject: Spanish
Topic: Literature

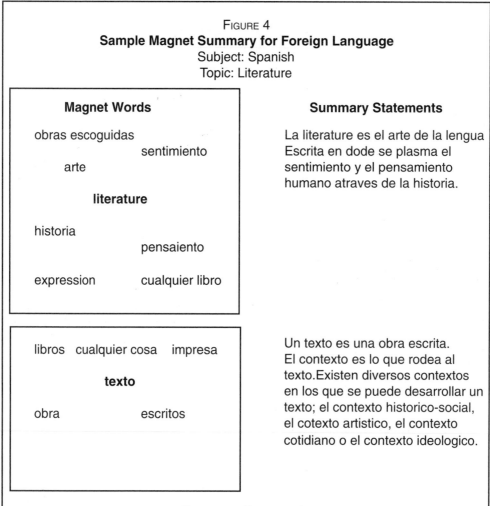

Magnet Words

obras escoguidas
sentimiento
arte

literature

historia
pensaiento

expression   cualquier libro

Summary Statements

La literature es el arte de la lengua
Escrita en dode se plasma el
sentimiento y el pensamiento
humano atraves de la historia.

libros   cualquier cosa   impresa

texto

obra   escritos

Un texto es una obra escrita.
El contexto es lo que rodea al
texto.Existen diversos contextos
en los que se puede desarrollar un
texto; el contexto historico-social,
el cotexto artistico, el contexto
cotidiano o el contexto ideologico.

Summary Paragraph

La literature es el arte de la lengua escrita en donde se plasma el pensamiento, el
sentimiento y la expresion humanas. Una pieze literaria es una obra escrita en
donde el texto se desarrolla alrededor de contextos. Los contextos pueden ser
historico-sociales, artisticos, ideologicos o cotidianos.

Special thanks to Carla Duran for contributing this example.

References

Anderson, T. H., & Armbruster, B. B. (1984). Studying. In P. D. Pearson (Ed.), *Handbook of reading research* (pp. 657-679). New York: Longman.

Buehl, D. (1995). *Classroom strategies for interactive learning.* Schofield, WS: Wisconsin State Reading Association.

Devine, T. G. (1991). Studying: Skills, strategies and systems. In J. Flood, J. M. Jensen, D. Lapp, & J. R. Squire (Eds.), *Handbook of research on teaching the English language arts* (pp. 743-753). New York: MacMillan.

Hill, M. (1991). Writing summaries promotes thinking and learning across the curriculum – but why are they so difficult to write? *Journal of Reading, 34,* 536-539.

Koskinen, P. S., Gambrell, L. B., Kapinus, B. A., & Heathington, B. S. (1988). Retelling: A strategy for enhancing students' reading comprehension. *The Reading Teacher, 41,* 892-896.

Palinscar, A. S., & Brown, A. L. (1983). *Reciprocal teaching of comprehension monitoring activities* (Technical Report No. 269). Champaign, Illinois, Center for the Study of Reading. (ERIC Document Reproduction Service No. ED 225 135).

Pincus, A., Geller, E. B., & Stover, E. M. (1986). A technique for using story schema as a transition to understanding and summarizing event-based magazine articles. *Journal of Reading, 30,* 152-158.

Searfoss, L. W., Readence, J. E., & Mallette, M. H. (2001). *Helping children learn to read: Creating a classroom literacy environment* (4th ed.). Boston: Allyn & Bacon.

Taylor, B. M. (1992). Text structure, comprehension, and recall. In S. J. Samuels & A. E. Farstrup (Eds.), *What research has to say about reading instruction* (pp. 220-235). Newark, DE: International Reading Association.

Wood, K. D. (1994) *Practical strategies for improving instruction.* Columbus, OH: National Middle School Association.

10

Helping Students Gain More Information from Textbooks

Research/Theory/Rationale. Research has shown that many textbooks used in our schools are not particularly well written, thereby causing students to have difficulty comprehending the textbooks intended for their grade level (Armbruster & Anderson, 1981). In these so-called "inconsiderate" or "unfriendly" texts, concepts may be presented in an unclear, illogical manner with either too much or not enough description and explanation (Armbruster, 1984). Finally, because the "comprehension" questions of a particular lesson often appear only at the end of textbook chapters, students do not learn their purposes for reading until after they have completed the assignment, despite the fact that research has shown that even good readers benefit when questions are interspersed throughout a text (Wood, 1986). One way to use questions during the reading of a selection is to develop study guides to accompany difficult chapters in textbooks (Wood, Lapp, & Flood, 1992). Study guides enable teachers to reduce the amount of print students must deal with at a given time by using questions interspersed throughout the text. Additionally, these guides can be developed to aid students' metacognitive abilities while they read, helping students vary their reading rate, monitor their comprehension, and focus on the most significant information in the text. The remainder of this chapter describes strategies for helping students gain more and better information as they read their textbooks through the use of various study guides.

INTERACTIVE READING GUIDE

The Interactive Reading Guide (Wood, 1988) is a teacher-directed guide designed to lead students through the reading of textbook material in an orchestral manner, sometimes requiring responses from individuals, small groups, pairs, or the whole class. At various points in their reading, students may be asked to predict what may occur next, develop associations, discuss a segment of information with a partner, read and retell content in their own words, or contribute their free recalls of the material to the class. Many of these responses require students to work collaboratively with one another, and nearly all of them elicit the development and use of higher-level thinking abilities, while engaging metacognitive strategies. Figure 1 (p. 81) is an example of an interactive reading guide for social studies on the topic of "The Arctic Region."

FIGURE 1
Interactive Reading Guide
The Arctic Region

Interaction Codes

Individual 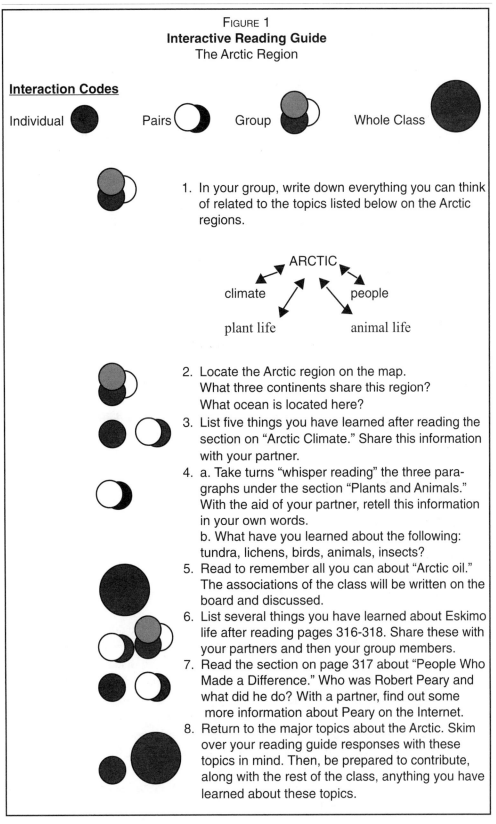   Pairs   Group   Whole Class

1. In your group, write down everything you can think of related to the topics listed below on the Arctic regions.

ARCTIC

climate   people

plant life   animal life

2. Locate the Arctic region on the map. What three continents share this region? What ocean is located here?

3. List five things you have learned after reading the section on "Arctic Climate." Share this information with your partner.

4. a. Take turns "whisper reading" the three paragraphs under the section "Plants and Animals." With the aid of your partner, retell this information in your own words.
   b. What have you learned about the following: tundra, lichens, birds, animals, insects?

5. Read to remember all you can about "Arctic oil." The associations of the class will be written on the board and discussed.

6. List several things you have learned about Eskimo life after reading pages 316-318. Share these with your partners and then your group members.

7. Read the section on page 317 about "People Who Made a Difference." Who was Robert Peary and what did he do? With a partner, find out some more information about Peary on the Internet.

8. Return to the major topics about the Arctic. Skim over your reading guide responses with these topics in mind. Then, be prepared to contribute, along with the rest of the class, anything you have learned about these topics.

Procedures
- Choose a chapter, literature selection, or portion of a chapter or story for study.
- Divide the textual material into manageable segments.
- Devise a series of questions and activities based on the information in the textbook. Focus on tasks that require students to go beyond what is stated explicitly in the text and ask them to "read between the lines" in their responses. (For example, use phrases such as "write down everything you can think of about…" or "jot down several things you have learned after reading…" Refer to Figure 1 for further examples.)
- Determine which activities might be accomplished by individuals, pairs, small groups, or the class as a whole. Again, consider which tasks might elicit quality responses, either through discussion in pairs or small groups or through whole class contributions. Some topics are especially valuable in creating "cognitive dissonance," which can spark high-caliber thoughts and passionate responses.

TEXTBOOK ACTIVITY GUIDE

Students who possess strong metacognitive abilities are able to relate prior knowledge to new information, can predict what might happen next, reread when something does not seem logical, evaluate the content of what was read, engage in self-questioning, and focus on the important portions of the text. These students approach the reading task as an active, dynamic process, while for students without these skills, reading is a passive activity involving minimal interaction and reader involvement (Baker & Brown, 1984). The *Textbook Activity Guide* (TAG) (Davey, 1986) can be a useful activity for students of varied ability levels who are not yet proficient in sound reading and study habits.

Procedures
Developing a TAG
- Select a portion of a textbook chapter which may cause students some difficulty when reading.
- Decide upon the significant concepts and determine the appropriate task for each concept. Davey (1986) suggests using semantic maps or diagrams when necessary to help organize information, or promoting discussion between two or more students when a critical analysis is required.
- Develop a strategy code and a self-monitoring code to assist students in the metacognitive process. These codes should be thoroughly explained and modeled to the students. Also, make certain that the codes are printed at the top of the guide for easy reference. (See Figure 2, p. 83, for an example of sample codes from Davey.)
- Design a guide that reflects your chapter objectives and is appropriate for the majority of students in your classroom.

FIGURE 2
Sample Strategy and Self-monitoring Codes
(Davey, 1986)

Strategy Codes

RR   *Read* and *retell* in your own words, taking turns with your partner.

PP   *Predict* with your *partner*.

WR   Provide a *written response* on your own and compare with
            your partner.

SKIM   Look at the purpose stated and read quickly. Afterwards, discuss
            with your partner.

MOC   Develop a semantic *map, outline*, or *chart* with your partner that
            depicts the information in this section.

Self-monitoring Codes

—   I understood this information.

?   I'm not certain if I understand.

X   I do not understand and I need to restudy.

Using the TAG

- Thoroughly explain, model, and demonstrate the strategy codes and self-monitoring codes by walking students through the guide. Discuss how it is often necessary to vary one's reading rate, and how to employ corrective (i.e., metacognitive) strategies based on the information presented and understanding of the text.
- Assign each student a partner. Pairing a student with someone who is slightly more proficient in reading can be advantageous for both learners.
- Monitor the students' progress and maintain the pace of the lesson by circulating around the room. Be prepared to offer assistance and clarification as necessary; it may be helpful to check students' understanding and use of self-monitoring codes as well.
- As students complete the guide, engage them in a discussion of the guide questions by asking them to show or tell what information led them to various answers or conclusions.
- Finally, help students become aware of how these reading and study strategies should be internalized and applied to other settings even when a TAG is not available.

Figures 3 (p. 84) and 4 (p. 86) are examples of TAGs.

FIGURE 3
Sample Textbook Activity Guide
World History: The African and Asian World

Names _____   Date(s)_____
          _____

Strategy Codes
RR	Read and retell in your own words
DP	Read and discuss with partner
PP	Predict with partner
WR	Write a response on your own
Skim	Read quickly for purpose stated and discuss with partner
MOC	Organize information with a map, chart, or outline

Self-monitoring Codes

___✓___   I understand this information

___?___   I'm not sure if I understand

___x___   I do not understand and I need to restudy

1. _____   DP   pp. 139-150. *Before* surveying the text with your partner, brainstorm about your existing knowledge on this topic. Jot down your ideas. Compare your responses *after* surveying the text

2. _____   WR   Jot down five or more vocabulary words and definitions for your collection.

3. _____   DP   pp. 139-140. In your own words, what are the five common characteristics of these countries?

4. _____   Skim   p. 140. How has oil caused conflict and change?

5. _____   WR   p. 140-141 – Iraq. Name three major facts you learned about Iraq.

6. _____   RR   p. 141-142 – Agriculture. Briefly summarize your retellings.

7. _____   DP   pp. 142-144 – Oil. How has oil production influenced life in Iraq?

8. _____   MOC   p. 143. Refer to the map at the bottom of p. 143. Make a graph depicting the major industry and resources in these countries.

(continued)

(Figure 3, continued)

9. _____ DP pp. 144-145 – Iran. React to the following and substantiate
                your responses.
                a. The Iranians welcomed foreigners.
                b. Khomeini favored progress and an emphasis on new
                    technology.

10. _____ RR p. 146. After reading and retelling, synthesize your
                 knowledge about a. land reform, b. production lands,
                 and c. manufacturing.

11. _____ MOC p. 146-148 – Saudi Arabia. Make a chart comparing and
                  contrasting the two groups in Saudi Arabia: the hadan and
                  the badia.

12. _____ DP pp. 148-150.
                 a. Write down some facts about the Arabian Peninsula
                    (Also, refer to map on p. 139).
                 b. What is the role of sheiks?
                 c. How did oil production change Saudi Arabia?

13. _____ MOC p. 150. After referring to the map on p. 134 and reading this
                  section, outline the three sections of the Arabian Borderlands.

FIGURE 4
Textbook Activity Guide
Earth Science: Fossils

Names _____   Date(s)_____

_____

Strategy Codes

RR	Read and retell in your own words
DP	Read and discuss with partner
PP	Predict with partner
WR	Write a response on your own
Skim	Read quickly for purpose stated and discuss with partner
MOC	Organize information with a map, chart, or outline

Self-monitoring Codes

✓   I understand this information

?   I'm not sure if I understand

x   I do not understand and I need to restudy

1. _____   PP   pp. 385-391. Survey the title, picture, charts, and headings. What do you expect to learn about this section?

2. _____   WR   As you are reading, jot down three or more new words and definitions for your vocabulary collection.

3. _____   RR   pp. 385-386 first three paragraphs.

4. _____   DP   pp. 386-387 next three paragraphs.
a. Describe several reasons why index or guide fossils are important.
b. How can finding the right type of fossil help you to identify it?

5. _____   MOC   Map pp. 387-388. Make an outline of the information.

6. _____   Skim   p. 390 first three paragraphs.
Purpose: To understand the role of the following in the formation of fossils _____ a. natural casts _____ b. trails and burrows _____ c. gastroliths

7. _____   DP   pp.390-391. As an amateur fossil collector describe:
a.where to find fossils; b.what to use to find them; c.how to prepare them for display.

8. _____   WR   p. 392 next to last paragraph. Define pseudofossil. Jot down three other words which contain the prefix "pseudo." Use the dictionary if necessary.

9. _____   DP   Examine the fossil collection being passed around and list eight things you have learned by analyzing it.

READING ROAD MAP

Numerous types of reading guides have been reported in professional literature, many of which are designed to intersperse questions throughout the selection to coordinate with topics and headings offered by the text. Described here is a version of the reading guide called the Reading Road Map (Wood, 1988). While good readers subconsciously know when to skim over material that is not significant, less proficient readers tend to read all textual material at the same rate – either too laboriously or too quickly and carelessly. By the use of "road signs" to depict reading speed, the Reading Road Map can help students learn to adjust their reading rates based on the different purposes for reading a particular passage. Figure 5 (p. 88) contains an excerpt from a Reading Road Map for a science chapter on pollution.

Procedures

Designing the Guide
- Decide on the most important information in the textbook chapter or literature selection.

- Begin the guide with a question designed to elicit the students' prior knowledge.

- Proceed sequentially by designing questions, activities, or statements that emphasize the significant concepts.

- Decide at each step how thoroughly the students should read each portion of the text, and insert the reading rate indicators accordingly.

- Conclude the map with an associational activity to encourage a mental review of the recently encountered concepts of "memories." Try to make the map and "journey" as realistic and relevant as possible.

Implementing the Guide
- Begin your implementation of the Reading Road Map by explaining the purposes of the assignment to the students. Discuss the idea of varying one's reading rate according to the purpose for reading. Be sure the students understand that the map is designed to guide them through the text by pointing out the most important concepts and events.
- Have the students skim the map and the text selection so they can "chart their course" and know where they are going before they get there.
- Work through the first few items as a class and model the expected answers.
- To make the map a cooperative activity, assign students a partner with whom they can work or "travel." They can take turns discussing their responses, reading and retelling passages of the text, and comparing the thinking behind their chosen answers.

- As individuals or pairs of students work on their guides, the teacher can circulate around the room to provide assistance and monitor student progress. At selected points in the lesson, the teacher can engage the learners in a class discussion of what has been completed so far.

FIGURE 5
Excerpt from a Reading Road Map for Science

Overall Mission: You are about to learn how air pollution, water pollution, and pesticides affect our lives.

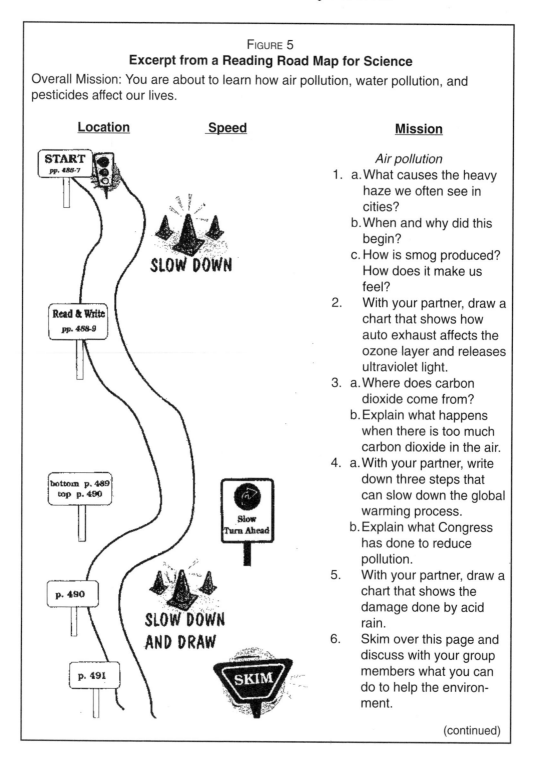

Location   **Speed**   **Mission**

START
pp. 488-7

SLOW DOWN

Read & Write
pp. 488-9

bottom p. 489
top p. 490

Slow
Turn Ahead

p. 490

SLOW DOWN
AND DRAW

p. 491

SKIM

Air pollution
1. a. What causes the heavy haze we often see in cities?
    b. When and why did this begin?
    c. How is smog produced? How does it make us feel?
2. With your partner, draw a chart that shows how auto exhaust affects the ozone layer and releases ultraviolet light.
3. a. Where does carbon dioxide come from?
    b. Explain what happens when there is too much carbon dioxide in the air.
4. a. With your partner, write down three steps that can slow down the global warming process.
    b. Explain what Congress has done to reduce pollution.
5. With your partner, draw a chart that shows the damage done by acid rain.
6. Skim over this page and discuss with your group members what you can do to help the environment.

(continued)

(Figure 5, continued)

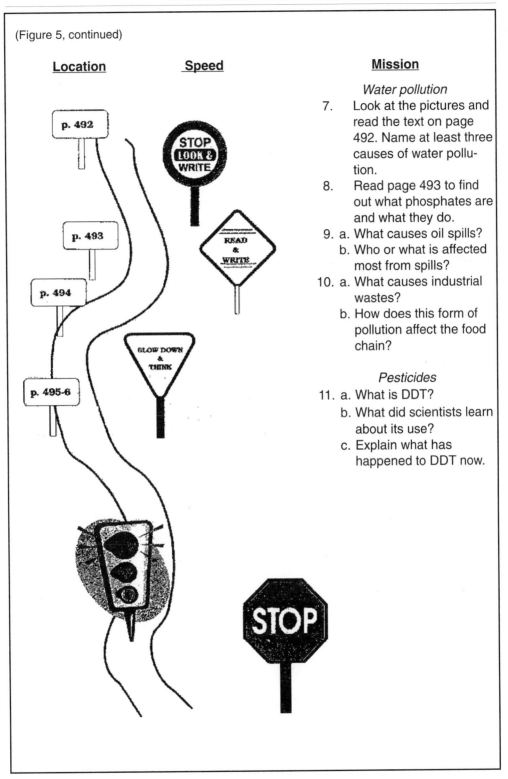

Location   **Speed**

Mission

Water pollution

7. Look at the pictures and read the text on page 492. Name at least three causes of water pollution.

8. Read page 493 to find out what phosphates are and what they do.

9. a. What causes oil spills?
   b. Who or what is affected most from spills?

10. a. What causes industrial wastes?
    b. How does this form of pollution affect the food chain?

Pesticides

11. a. What is DDT?
    b. What did scientists learn about its use?
    c. Explain what has happened to DDT now.

POINT OF VIEW READING GUIDE

Studies have shown that asking readers to change their perspective to coordinate with the content of reading material can improve comprehension and recall by activating specific dimensions of their prior knowledge or schemata (Anderson & Pichert, 1978; Anderson, Pichert & Shirey, 1983; Pichert & Anderson, 1977). One method for strategically leading students to broaden their perspective while reading subject area material is the Point of View Reading Guide (Wood, 1988). With the guide to lead them, readers essentially take on the schemata of another individual. Thus, readers become personally involved with the content, which in turn can enhance their comprehension and recall. The Point of View Reading Guide engages students in a critical and creative thinking exercise and a writing activity while simultaneously helping them recall and assimilate new information. Also, responding to expository or narrative material in dialogue format can be stimulating both affectively and cognitively.

Procedures
- Provide an initial statement to develop the readers' mental set by telling them that they are about to be interviewed as if they were a character in the text. (See Figures 6, 7, and 8, pp. 91-92)
- Design a series of sequentially ordered questions to which students must respond during reading. By doing so, the questions themselves help to divide the material into manageable sections.
- Structure the questions so that students change their perspective and take on the point view of a character, animal, plant, or object being studied in the text. Use the "interview" format when developing the questions so that they elicit elaborate responses from the students.
- A first question such as, "What do you look like?" gives the students an opportunity to use their imaginations to embellish upon the explicit information provided by the textbook. Subsequent questions enable the learners to feel each of the experiences encountered and to describe them from the first person point of view.
- In order to answer the interview questions, encourage students to combine information from pictures, diagrams, charts, maps, text, and most importantly, their heads.

FIGURE 6
Point of View Reading Guide
English/Language Arts
Rikki-Tikki-Tavi by Rudyard Kipling

Imagine that you are Rikki-Tikki-Tavi being interviewed by reporters over the telephone. Answer the following interview questions.

1. Since we are not there in person to see you ourselves, please, Mr. Tavi, tell us what you look like.

2. Mr. Tavi, how did you come to live with Teddy's family after all?

3. What was your first night in a strange place like?

4. How did you feel the first time you saw Nag? Describe Nag for us.

5. What was your reaction when you heard Nag and Nagaina plotting to kill the people you live with?

6. It must have been a very tense moment when you found Nagaina ready to strike at Teddy. How did you manage to divert her attention?

A special thanks to teacher Susan Avett for developing this guide.

FIGURE 7
Point of View Reading Guide
Science: Fungi

Imagine that you are being interviewed by reporters for a television documentary. Write down in dialogue form your responses to their questions. Remember to use the information in your book as a guide.

p. 34   1. Tell us about yourself and your family. How would we know if we saw you somewhere?

Well, we're plant-like consumers, you know. In other words, we eat other things. We all have your basic cell wall and nucleus (our control centers). You've probably met our cousins—mold, mildew, yeast, and mushrooms.

p. 34   2. We hear you do a lot of good out there for man and the environment. Please, tell us how.

Gosh, well we're used in the food industry quite a bit. The mushrooms over there get fried and eaten with steak. Some of us look like mushrooms, but you wouldn't eat us, we're poisonous. Yeast causes bread to rise and is used to make vitamins. Some medicines are even made from our cousin, Penicillin.

(continued)

(Figure 7, continued)

p. 35   3. We also hear you have a negative side as well. Tell us about it.

Well, okay, okay. We'll tell. We mostly go after things made by other organisms like cotton, cloth or leather and we try to break them down. We even like plastic sometimes. We cause fruit to spoil and smell bad and bread to get moldy when it's left out. We don't like cool, dry, places though.

p. 35   4. That's not all, what about your role in diseases?

All right, so we cause ringworm and athlete's foot. (That's a disease you can get in the locker room if you're not careful). We also go after plants and corn, causing corn smut.

FIGURE 8 *
Point of View History Guide
Chapter 11: The War of 1812

You are about to be interviewed as if you were a person living in the United States in the early 1800s. Describe your reactions to each of the following events.

Planting the Seeds of War (p. 285)
    I.   As a merchant in a coastal town, tell why your business is doing poorly.

The War Debate (pp. 285-287)
    2.   Explain why you decided to become a war hawk. Who was your leader?
    3.   Tell why many of your fellow townspeople lowered their flags at half mast.
    4.   What was the reaction of Great Britain to you and your people at that time?
    5.   In your opinion, is America ready to fight? Explain why you feel this way.

Perry's Victory (p. 287)
    6.   In what ways were your predictions either correct or incorrect about America's willingness to fight this war?
    7.   Tell about your experiences under Captain Perry's command.

Death of Tecumseh (p. 288)
    8.   Mr. Harrison, describe what really happened near the Thames River in Canada.
    9.   What was Richard Johnson's role in that battle?
    10.   Now, what are your future plans?

Death of the Creek Confederacy (p. 288)
    11.   Explain how your people, the Cherokees, actually helped the United States.
    12.   Tell about your leader.

British Invasion (pp. 288-289)
    13.   As a British soldier, what happened when you got to Washington, D.C.?
    14.   You headed to Fort McHenry after Washington. What was the outcome?
    15.   General Jackson, it's your turn. Tell about your army and how you defeated the British in New Orleans.

The Treaty of Ghent (p. 290)
    16.   We will end our interview with some final observations from the merchant questioned earlier. We will give you some names of people. Tell how they are now that the war is over: the British, the Indians, the United States, Harrison, and Jackson.

*Reprinted with permission of Karen D. Wood and the International Reading Association.

Requirements for the Implementation of the Point of View Guide

- *Model and demonstrate*
  Encountering the interview-type questions suggested here will likely cause some confusion unless their purpose is explained in advance. Give the class one or more sample responses orally or graphically. Show the students how such a response may require that they infer information from the text and use elaborations of their own.
- *Group students*
  Consider allowing students to work in pairs or small groups to complete the guide. Often, working in groups reduces the risk of offering unusual responses and permits students to be more creative and true to the assignment. Make certain that students are grouped heterogeneously so that all can benefit from the experience.
- *Praise creativity*
  Encourage creative responses through acceptance and praise. As they engage in their dialogue, have the students use written punctuation, interjections, cliches, stammering, or whatever might realistically portray the desired emotion.

Suggestions for the Use of Reading Guides

The following guidelines may be useful in the development and implementation of any study guide, including the reading guides suggested here (Wood, Lapp, & Flood, 1992).

- *Build in a review of the content.*
  Ask students to think back over specific topics from their reading. Such an activity forces a mental and/or written review of newly learned information, thereby enhancing comprehension and retention.
- *Use creativity in designing the guide.*
  Anything that deviates from the traditional sheet with questions is more likely to arouse the interest of even the most reluctant student, so use a variety of shapes, sketches, or even colors when designing your guide.
- *Allow students to work together.*
  Students who may experience difficulty can be grouped with those slightly more proficient so that all may contribute to the varying degrees of expertise and benefit from the experience.
- *Have students survey both the text and the guide.*
  This survey step helps students establish a mental set of expectations for the new content to be presented; additionally, this activity leads them on the way to an effective method of studying independently.
- *Explain the purposes and model the procedures before beginning.*
  It is essential that students understand that the guide is intended to help them focus on the important information in the text. It is also helpful to work through several of the items as a class to ensure a thorough understanding of how the guide works.

- *Continually monitor student progress.*
  As the class is working through the guide, the teacher should circulate around the room to clarify points, answer questions, and monitor progress.
- *Include a class discussion after completion.*
  A reading guide is an excellent vehicle to stimulate discussion and promote student-to-teacher interaction.
- *Avoid assigning grades.*
  Reading guides need not be graded in the traditional sense. As the name implies, the purpose is to serve as a guide, not a test, on the written material. Consequently, a mark indicating completion should be sufficient for grading purposes.
- *Do not overuse the reading guide concept.*
  Like any new strategy, the reading guide can lose its novelty and effectiveness if used too frequently. It is best to choose chapters or selections that may be difficult for students to understand due to the material's dense construction or stylistic presentation.
- *Help students become independent learners.*
  The ultimate goal of all instruction is to enable students to develop the skills and strategies necessary to learn on their own. Students should be shown that the strategies learned and practiced through the reading guide can be applied to the reading of any new material.

References

Anderson, R. C., & Pichert, J. W. (1978). Recall of previously unrecallable information following a shift in perspective. *Journal of Verbal Learning and Verbal Behavior, 17,* 1-12.

Anderson, R. C., Pichert, J. W., & Shirey, L. L. (1983). Effects of the readers' schema at different points in time. *Journal of Educational Psychology, 75,* 271-279.

Armbruster, B. B. (1984). The problem of "inconsiderate text." In G. Duffy, R. Roehler, & J. Mason (Eds.), *Comprehension instruction: Perspectives and suggestions* (pp. 202-217). New York: Longman.

Armbruster, B. B., & Anderson, T. H. (1981). Content area textbooks. *Reading Educational Report No. 23.* Champaign, IL: Center for the Study of Reading.

Baker, L., & Brown, A. L. (1984). Metacognitive skills and reading. In P. D. Pearson (Ed.), *Handbook of reading research* (pp.353-394). New York: Longman.

Davey, B. (1986). Using textbook activity guides to help students learn from textbooks. *Journal of Reading, 29,* 489-494.

Pichert, J. W., & Anderson, R. C. (1977). Taking different perspectives on a story. *Journal of Educational Psychology, 69,* 309-315.

Wood, K. D. (1986). The effect of interspersing questions in text: Evidence for "slicing the task". *Reading Research and Instruction, 25,* 295-307.

Wood, K. D. (1988). Guiding students through informational text. *The Reading Teacher, 41,* 912-920.

Wood, K. D., Lapp, D., & Flood, J. (1992). *Guiding readers through text: A review of study guides.* Newark, DE: International Reading Association.

11

Asking Questions That Promote Understanding

Research/Theory/Rationale. Teachers in all content areas and at all grade levels use questions to guide comprehension. Questions promote cognitive support at many levels, such as helping students recall important information, analyze, synthesize, and evaluate ideas, and even interpret ideas in new ways (Graves, Juel, & Graves, 2000). Yet, many students do not know where to find the answers to questions and therefore need explicit support from the teacher. Students can benefit from instruction that helps them develop an awareness of how to find the answers to specific types of questions. This chapter describes a strategy, entitled Question-Answer Relationships, that explains how to find the answers to different questions. Another strategy described in this chapter is Questioning the Author, a whole-class discussion framework that uses questions called queries to guide students as they construct meaning from texts.

QUESTION-ANSWER RELATIONSHIPS

Raphael and Pearson (1982) developed the Question-Answer Relationship or QAR program to teach students strategies for answering questions. This program is derived from the work of Pearson and Johnson (1978) who developed a system for classifying questions based on a three-way relationship between the question, the information in the text, and the preexisting knowledge of the reader. They suggested that a question can be classified as one of the following: (1) ***textually explicit*** in which the answer is explicitly stated in the text and requires little thinking on the part of the student; (2) ***textually implicit*** in which the answer is implied in the text and students must search for ideas that are related to each other and put them together to answer the question; and (3) ***scriptally implicit*** in which the reader must rely on background knowledge or prior experience to answer the question. Based on this classification system, a question-answering strategy, entitled Question-Answer Relationships, has proven to be effective in teaching students about sources of information for answering comprehension questions (Raphael, 1982, 1984, 1986; Raphael & Pearson, 1982). Corresponding with Pearson and Johnson's (1978) system of classifying questions described above, students can be taught four types of QARs. The types of questions and how they correspond with other familiar terms such as literal, synthesis, inferential, and critical/creative are shown in Figure 1 (p. 96). Notice how the terminology used in this training program is appropriate for students and how it helps them to distinguish among the sources for different answers.

"Right There/In the Text"

The answer is located on the page. It is on the lines. Words from the question and words from the answer are clearly stated in the book.

"Think and Search/Search the Text"

The answer is harder to find. You might have to look in more than one sentence and piece the information together. The answer is in the text, but the reader must search various parts of the text and synthesize the information. It is "between the lines."

"Author and You/Reader and Author"

The answer is not in the text. The reader must use prior knowledge as well as what the author says to answer the question.

"On My Own/In the Reader's Head"

The answer is not found right in the book. You must find it in your head and use what you already know. The text stimulates the reader's thinking, but the answer is based on the reader's own experiences and knowledge. The answer is "beyond the lines."

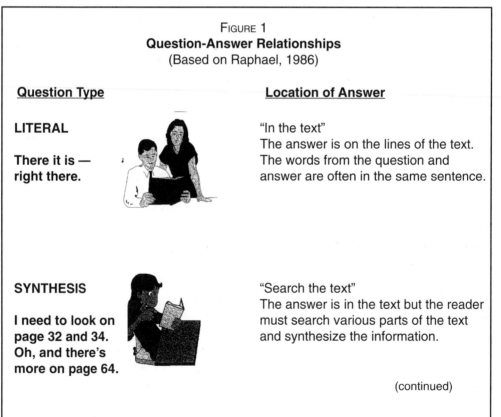

FIGURE 1
Question-Answer Relationships
(Based on Raphael, 1986)

Question Type		Location of Answer
LITERAL **There it is — right there.**		"In the text" The answer is on the lines of the text. The words from the question and answer are often in the same sentence.
SYNTHESIS **I need to look on page 32 and 34. Oh, and there's more on page 64.**		"Search the text" The answer is in the text but the reader must search various parts of the text and synthesize the information.

(continued)

(Figure 1, continued)

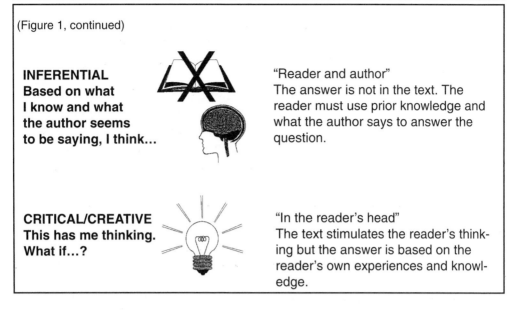

INFERENTIAL
Based on what
I know and what
the author seems
to be saying, I think...

"Reader and author"
The answer is not in the text. The
reader must use prior knowledge and
what the author says to answer the
question.

CRITICAL/CREATIVE
This has me thinking.
What if...?

"In the reader's head"
The text stimulates the reader's thinking but the answer is based on the
reader's own experiences and knowledge.

Procedures

- Introduce the students to the QAR terms and concepts. Use one or two
  sentence examples along with questions and answers for each category with
  the QARs already labeled. Discuss how each fits into the corresponding
  categories.

Example

Text: *The farmer gazed at his empty thermos and started back.*
He was more tired than usual today.

Right There: What object caught the farmer's eye? *(the empty thermos)*
Think and Search: Why did the farmer start back? *(his thermos was empty*
and he was thirsty; he was more tired than usual)
Author and You: Why would an empty thermos make the farmer leave?
(he was thirsty and tired and wanted to get something else to drink)
What do you suppose was in the thermos? *(something hot like coffee;*
something cold)
Where was the farmer before he left? *(since he is a farmer, he is*
probably out in a field)
On My Own: Use your imagination to describe the scene.
What are some possible things the farmer could be raising?
(many answers are possible for these two questions)

- Again present students with a short passage with questions and answers but
  have them identify the QAR.
- Give students the passages and questions and have them read and decide
  which of the QAR strategies is needed by writing their responses on paper.
- Increase the length of the passage to approximately 75 to 100 words and

increase the number of questions to five. Allow students to work through one passage as a class, then gradually release the responsibility to them in small groups, pairs, then individually; continually circulate among the groups to monitor student progress.

- Increase the passage to a full length text selection or story.
- Generalize the strategy to other materials, such as newspaper articles, films, and other subject areas (this is especially appropriate in the case of interdisciplinary teaming). The illustration in Figure 2 shows how the system of classifying question-answer relationships can be applied to content areas such a science.

FIGURE 2
Sample QARs for Science
Science QARs

Text: *A solar eclipse occurs when Earth moves into the Moon's shadow. If Earth moves into the Moon's umbra, a total solar eclipse occurs.*

Right There or Textually Explicit
Q.What happens when the Earth moves into the Moon's shadow?
A. A solar eclipse occurs.

Think and Search or Textually Implicit
Q. During a solar eclipse where is the Moon in relationship to the Earth and the Sun?
A. It is between the Earth and the Sun, because the Earth is in the Moon's umbra or shadow.

Author and You or Textually Implicit
Q. What is the environment like during a total solar eclipse?
A. It is dark and cold.

On my Own or Scriptally Implicit
Q. What do you suppose would happen to the Earth if a total solar eclipse should remain for several months?
A. Numerous answers are possible here.

QUESTIONING THE AUTHOR

Questioning the Author (QTA) is a whole-class discussion approach used to support student interaction and engagement with narrative and expository texts (Beck, McKeown, Hamilton, & Kucan, 1997). Teachers explain to students that textbooks are written by authors who sometimes do not clearly explain an idea or concept. It is the responsibility of the reader to determine what the author is trying to say. Since the goal is to understand text ideas, teachers do not encourage students to offer opinions or personal connections but rather to maintain a focus on questioning and clarifying what the author has written. With this framework, teachers use specific questions called *queries* to help students construct meanings during the initial reading of the text. The procedures are presented in three parts: (1) planning, (2) discussing, and (3) implementing.

Procedures
Planning
- Read the text you would like the students to read. Identify the major ideas students will need to construct, and determine potential problems they may have with these ideas.
- Decide on strategic stopping points in the text for holding a class discussion. In other words, segment the text where there might be some confusion or where the author has addressed an important idea. These segments may be single sentences or whole paragraphs.
- For each segment, write suitable queries to help students construct meaning. Queries are questions that are designed to assist students as they grapple with text ideas during reading. They differ from questions used after reading that typically assess student comprehension. There are different kinds of queries, including initiating queries and follow-up queries. Initiating queries are discussion starters that help students focus on the main ideas of the passage. Examples are (Beck, McKeown, Hamilton, & Kucan, 1997):
  > What is the author trying to say here?
  > What is the author's message?
  > What is the author talking about? (p. 34)

Follow-up queries give direction to the discussion and help students make connections, make inferences, and draw conclusions as they construct meaning with the text. Examples are (Beck, McKeown, Hamilton, & Kucan, 1997):
> What does the author mean here?
> Does the author explain this clearly?
> Does this make sense with what the author told us before?
> How does this connect to what the author told us here?
> Does the author tell us why?
> Why do you think the author tells us this now? (pp. 37-38)

Discussing
- Begin the discussion with an initiating query.
- Encourage students to share their thoughts about the text.
- Use other discussion moves to keep the students engaged with the text. Beck and associates (1997) describe the following moves:

Marking: Draw attention to a student comment by restating it and highlighting its importance.
Example: "So President Lincoln was not going to change his mind."

Turning back: Direct students to look back at the text for clarification instead of giving the students answers.
Example: "Is that really what happened? Wait, I thought that ... Let's look again to see what the author said."

Revoicing: Help students articulate their responses if they are having difficulty putting their thoughts into words.
Example: "So in other words, …what you are saying is…"

Modeling: Model how to grapple with a difficult or confusing passage.
Example: "When I first read this paragraph, I thought something was wrong because …Then I reread and thought about…"

Annotating: Offer information that students need to understand a text idea.
Example: "One thing the author did not tell us is that .."

Recapping: Gather previously mentioned ideas to summarize what the students have discussed thus far.
Example: "Now we know why …Let's continue and we might find out…"

Implementing
- Arrange the room in a way to facilitate discussion.
- Inform the students that this discussion will be different from other class discussions.
- Make it clear to the students that authors are not perfect and that their writing may not be as clear as it should be. As readers, the students must figure out what the author is trying to say. Students who struggle can view their inability to make sense of text as not necessarily their fault. In this way, they may be more apt to participate in discussions to construct some understanding of the text ideas.

References

Beck, I., McKeown, M., Hamilton, R., & Kucan, L. (1997). *Questioning the author*. Newark, DE: International Reading Association.

Graves, M. F., Juel, C., & Graves, B. B. (2000). *Teaching reading in the 21st century* (2nd ed.). Boston: Allyn & Bacon.

Pearson, P. D., & Johnson, D. D. (1978). *Teaching reading comprehension*. New York: Holt, Rinehart, and Winston.

Raphael, T. E. (1982). Question-answering strategies for children. *The Reading Teacher, 26,* 186-190.

Raphael, T. E. (1984). Teaching learners about sources of information for answering comprehension questions. *Journal of Reading, 27,* 303-311.

Raphael, T. E. (1986) Teaching question-answer relationships, revisted. *The Reading Teacher,* 39, 6, 516-523.

Raphael, T. E., & Pearson, P. D. (1982). *The effect of metacognitive awareness training on children's question-and-answering behavior.* Technical Report #238. Urbana, IL: Center for the Study of Reading. University of Illinois.

12

Improving Students' Ability to Read Critically

Research/Theory/Rationale. Researchers, educators, and psychologists have long proclaimed the need to teach students how to analyze critically and "think beyond the lines" when engaged in learning (Goodman, 1992; Weaver & Alvermann, 2000). Traditionally, the problem has been how to do this within the constraints of prescribed content. One way is through the use of anticipation or reaction guides. These guides can be applied to a textbook chapter, unit or segment, or to a demonstration, class lecture, listening, or viewing assignment. They work equally well in all subject areas, and offer a way for teachers to promote transfer of the skill of critical thinking to other contexts. Another way to help students read critically is through writing. The use of writing as a powerful tool in learning has gained attention as a "way of knowing" in all disciplines and is supported by various professional organizations (National Council of Teachers of English, 1996; National Council of Teachers of Mathematics, 1998; National Research Council, 1996). Writing involves critical thinking and thus enhances learning in all subject areas. The critical thinking and reasoning needed to problem solve in mathematics and science also can be fostered with specific writing approaches designed to help students engage in both cognitive and metacognitive processes to extend their thinking. This chapter also describes an approach called *cubing* that helps students articulate their thinking and enhance their conceptual understanding.

REACTION GUIDE

The Reaction Guide (Readence, Bean, & Baldwin, 1998) is comprised of generalized, somewhat ambiguous statements to which students are asked to respond both before and after reading the related assignment. The result is a class of students who are engaged in active discussion and have broadened their learning or changed their point of view in a motivating and socially rewarding manner.

Procedures
   Designing the Guide
   • Begin by analyzing the unit of study for its most significant concepts. It is often helpful to choose topics that reflect typical misconceptions.
   • Develop no more than ten statements and present them in a thought-provoking manner.

- Include a column for responding both before and after the lesson. Or, as shown in some of the figures to follow, a column can be included for what the "author" was trying to say.

Implementing the Guide
- Distribute copies of the statements to the students and display the guide on an overhead, poster, or chalkboard.
- Arrange the students in pairs or small groups and tell them to take turns reading each of the statements to their partners.
- Ask the students to decide if they agree or disagree with the statements (they do not have to agree with each other), they should explain to others why and how they arrived at such a decision. ***This is essential to the success of the reaction guide because it encourages students to discuss the topic as they substantiate their responses, even if they are only making guesses about the content and meaning.***
- Then, engage in a whole class discussion, eliciting responses from the class. It is especially beneficial to have students cite examples from the text, video, or selection to indicate how they have broadened their thinking or changed their point of view.
- The teacher should circulate around the room to monitor progress and help students clarify their thinking.
- Next, the teacher conducts an informal poll to tally how many students agreed or disagreed with each statement. A nonjudgmental posture at this point will help the learners feel more comfortable with their divergent opinions.
- After the discussion, have the students read/listen/view the selection on which the guide is based. The targeted material could be a content area reading selection, a newspaper article, a short story, or a video. Instruct them to use these statements as guides to the reading, focusing on the key concepts reflected in the reaction guide as they read.
- Tell the students to read the selection on their own using the statements as their guide. Ask them to make mental or written notes of the new and relevant information.
- The students should then return to their groups to discuss each statement again, responding, and sometimes revising, in the "after" column of the guide.
- Then, engage in a whole class discussion, eliciting responses from the class. It is especially beneficial to have students cite examples from the text, video, or selection to indicate how they have broadened their thinking or changed their point of view. The teacher then calls on class members to add their new knowledge to the concepts by elaborating or substantiating their responses. In this step, the students are required to provide evidence (from the text) to support their answers.

Following are several examples of reaction guides applied to a short story in literature, a novel in an English class, a social studies lesson on the Nile River, and a science lesson on air (Figures 1-4, pp. 103-105).

FIGURE 1
Sample Reaction Guide/Literature:
"Seventh Grade" by Gary Soto

Directions: Take turns reading each of these statements with your partner. In the "Before" column, put a "+" (plus) if you agree with the statement or a "-" (minus) if you disagree. Make sure you justify your reactions with personal experiences, ideas, events, or analogies. After reading, return to the statements by marking what the author/story says and indicate in the "After" column if you have changed your mind or broadened your views.

Before	Statement	After Author	After You
—	1. When you like someone, you sometimes do unusual things.	—	—
—	2. Sometimes people go to extremes to make a good impression.	—	—
—	3. Being yourself always pays off in the end.	—	—
—	4. Others can always see through you if you are not being yourself.	—	—

FIGURE 2
Sample Reaction Guide/English:
The Gift of the Magi by O. Henry

Directions: Take turns reading each statement aloud with the person seated next to you. Mark with a plus or minus in the "before" column if you agree or disagree with the statement. You do not have to agree with your partner, but make sure you substantiate your response. After reading the story, return to the guide, reread your statements, and mark in the "after" column to see if you have changed your mind or broadened your view.

Before		After	Author
—	1. You should always strive to make your life better.	—	—
—	2. Love is unselfish.	—	—
—	3. When it comes to giving gifts, it is the thought that counts.	—	—
—	4. A true gift requires sacrifice.	—	—
—	5. Gifts should always be useful to the receiver.	—	—
—	6. Pride in material possessions is misplaced.	—	—

FIGURE 3
Sample Reaction Guide/Social Studies:
The Nile River Basin

Before		After
_____	1. The Nile is one of the longest rivers in the world.	_____
_____	2. Long ago, the Nile was helpful in making the region around it prosperous.	_____
_____	3. The Nile runs through Morocco, Algeria, Libya, and Egypt.	_____
_____	4. The presence of the Aswan Dam has been most beneficial to the people of Egypt.	_____
_____	5. The flooding of the Nile has always brought disaster to the people of the basin region.	_____
_____	6. There is more than one Nile river in Africa.	_____

Figure 4
Sample Reaction Guide/Earth Science:
Air

Before   After

_____ 1. The earth's atmosphere is made up of gases and liquids.   _____

_____ 2. Nitrogen is taken in directly as a food source for plants and animals.   _____

_____ 3. Without carbon dioxide, plants could not produce oxygen.   _____

_____ 4. The atmosphere is made up of two layers.   _____

_____ 5. The ozone layer keeps ultraviolet radiation from reaching
the earth's surface.   _____

_____ 6. The coldest layer of the atmosphere is the stratosphere.   _____

_____ 7. Barometers measure the force and direction of air.   _____

Figure 5 (p. 106) is a sample of a reaction guide for chemistry which can be used before and after the reading or just after the reading as a review of key concepts. As shown here, another adaptation of the original reaction guide format requires that students write why they agree or disagree with the statement, providing yet another way to "smuggle" writing across the curriculum.

EXTENDED ANTICIPATION/REACTION GUIDE

The Extended Anticipation Guide (Duffelmeyer, 1994; Duffelmeyer & Baum, 1992) is similar to the Reaction Guide described above; however, as the name implies, this strategy *extends* students' thinking by adding another component to the activity. After determining their initial beliefs in the pre-reading stage, a second set of questions allows students to decide whether or not the text supports their choices from the original guide. If the support does not exist, students are asked to summarize and paraphrase the text thus enabling them to retain the new information, begin thinking critically, and improve their reading skills.

Procedures
Preparing the Guide
- Decide on a story, textbook selection, or other material to be studied, and note the key concepts and lesson objectives.

FIGURE 5
Sample Reaction Guide/Chemistry:

Directions: With your partner, read through each statement and discuss why you either agree or disagree with the statements. We will engage in a whole class discussion of your thinking and predictions. Then read pages 322-345 in your chemistry textbook using these statements as your guide. After completing the reading, return to these statements and circle whether you agree or disagree with each and in the space provided, explain your answer. Be sure to cite page numbers that support your response.

1. *Changes that produce a new kind of matter with different properties are called chemical changes.* I agree/I disagree because_____

_____

2. *Physical changes do not produce new kinds of matter.* I agree/I disagree because _____

_____

3. *Properties, such as density, can be used to identify matter.* I agree/I disagree because _____

_____

4. *Matter cannot change from one state (solid, liquid, and gas) to another depending on the temperature.* I agree/I disagree because_____

_____

5. *A molecule is the largest particle of a substance that retains all of the properties of the substance and is composed of two or more atoms.* I agree/I disagree because_____

_____

6. *An atom is the smallest unit of matter.* I agree/I disagree because _____

_____

7. *Compounds can exist as solids, liquids, and gases.* I agree/I disagree because

_____

_____

8. *Compounds are made of elements in definite proportions.* I agree/I disagree because _____

_____

9. *Elements contain several kinds of atoms.* I agree/I disagree because _____

_____

10. *The release of a gas is evidence that a physical change has occurred.* I agree/I disagree because _____

_____

A special thanks to teacher, Sarah Agee, for contributing this example.

- Develop approximately five to ten statements that reflect these key concepts. Make certain that the statements are general in nature and are likely to stimulate students' thinking.
- Type or write the statements in the form of the guide and distribute copies to the class.

Pre-reading Stage
- Model the use of the guide by displaying it on an overhead projector. Explain to the students that it will improve their understanding by helping them remember what they know about the topic and allowing them to make predictions before they read.
- Assign each student a partner and ask the pairs to take turns reading the statements to each other, marking whether they agree or disagree. They do not have to agree with each other, but it is essential that they substantiate their responses.
- The teacher may choose to engage the whole class in a discussion of the answers in order to assess the level of prior knowledge or the degree of commonly held misconceptions on the topic. Explain to the students that they are free to share their individual thinking at this point in the lesson.

Reading Stage
- Have the students read the related text using the statements as a guide to the key concepts in the selection.

Post-reading Stage
- After reading the text selection, the students should indicate with a checkmark if they did or did not find information in the text to support their responses from the Pre-reading Stage.
- Finally, in the paraphrasing step, students have another opportunity to substantiate their answers. If they respond "Yes, the text supports my choice," the students write in column A (see Figure 6, p. 108) why their choice was correct. If the checked response is "No, there is no support in the text for my choice," the students should indicate in column B why their answer was inappropriate and summarize the correct information from the text.
- Again, the teacher may choose to hold a class discussion on the results of the activity in order to reinforce the key concepts of the lesson; and emphasize how the reading guide could be used as a guide in the Reading Stage.

FIGURE 6
Extended Anticipation/Reaction Guide
Earth Science

Part 1
Directions: *Take turns reading each statement in Part I with your partner. If you believe the statement is TRUE, put a check in the "Agree" column. If you believe it is FALSE, check the "Disagree" column. Be ready to explain your answer to each other and the class.*

Agree	Disagree	
		I. There are over a million types of life forms on Earth.
		2. Rain forests contain half of all the species on Earth.
		3. The destruction of rain forests can cause the Earth to get warmer.
		4. New laws have stopped people from hunting our wild animals.
		5. We throw enough garbage away each year to circle the earth with garbage trucks.
		6. People are recycling more today than they used to.

Part 2
Directions: *If the information supports your previous choice, put a check in the SUPPORT column. Briefly explain your decision in the appropriate WHY IS MY CHOICE CORRECT? column. If the information you read does not suport your first choice, put a check in the NO SUPPORT column and explain in the WHY IS MY CHOICE INCORRECT? column. Be sure to write your explanations in your own words, based on the information in the text.*

	Support	No Support	Why is my choice correct?	Why is my choice incorrect?
I.	✓		*Estimates of over 100 million counting tropics*	
2.		✓		*Rain forests cover 7% of land but have over 50% of species*
3.	✓		*Carbon from burning forests means global warming.*	
4.	✓		*People still kill for money, ivory, furs, research*	
5.		✓		*Garbage trucks could circle earth five times!*
6.		✓		*Estimates of over 60% of cans are recycled.*

REACTION REVIEW GUIDE

Another type of reaction guide which could be termed the Reaction Review Guide (Wood, 1992) can be used *after* the reading or study of a unit of instruction. The Reaction Review Guide, as the name implies, helps students synthesize what they have learned by responding to key statements and determining if they do or do not reflect the actual information in the unit, chapter, selection. Students (in pairs or alone) can refer back to their texts or notes for support if necessary and include a written response to the statement either agreeing or disagreeing with its premise. Some teachers have chosen to use the Reaction Review Guide as a quiz to determine what students have learned. The sample guide shown in Figure 7 illustrates how the Reaction Review Guide can be used to integrate writing with the study of mathematics in a middle grade classroom. Figure 8 (p. 110) shows how the Reaction Review Guide is applied to a geometry lesson in a high school classroom.

FIGURE 7
Sample Reaction Guide
Mathematics: Area and Perimeter
Names of Group Members
John H., Kara T.

Directions: With your partner, take turns reading and discussing each of the statements below. Put a check if you agree or disagree with each statement. Be sure to support your answer with at least one example. Use your book or any other sources for support.

1. An example of when you may need to know the perimeter would be if you were building a pen for your dog.
   __X__ I agree   _____ I disagree because: *You don't what to cover up the dog. You want to build the pen around him.*

2. To find the perimeter of an object you multiply all four sides.
   _____ I agree   __X__ I disagree because: *You want to find the distance around an object, not the inside.*
   Page 388 says perimeter is the distance around a figure.

3. We would need to know the area of our classroom if we were going to carpet the room.
   __X__ I agree   _____ I disagree because: *You want to carpet the whole floor not just the outside border.*

4. To find the area, you multiply all four sides together.
   _____ I agree   __X__ I disagree because: *You don't want to multiply 4 sides. Only multiply two side.- length x width. (p 394).*

5. There are many examples of how people use area in everyday life.
   __X__ I agree   _____ I disagree because: *The carpenters have to carpet the whole house, and the builders have to build the inside of the house too.*

A special thanks to teacher, Suzanne Billips, for contributing this guide.

Figure 8
Sample Reaction Guide
Geometry Unit

Directions: In your groups, take turns reading and discussing each of the statements below. Check whether you agree or disagree with each statement. Be sure to support your answer with at least one example. Use your book or any other sources for support.

1. There are always two different names for a triangle.
   I agree ✓   I disagree __   because: *You can look at the angles and name a triangle right, acute, or obtuse. Also, you can look at the sides of the triangle and name it equilateral, isosceles, or scalene.*

2. All of the angles of a triangle must be acute in order for a triangle to be an acute triangle.
   I agree ✓   I disagree __   because: *That is the definition of an acute triangle. The definition is that all of the angles of the triangle must be acute in order for the triangle to be an acute triangle. So the angles all have to be little angles, less than 90°.*

3. All of the angles of a triangle must be obtuse in order for a triangle to be an obtuse triangle.
   I agree __   I disagree ✓   because: *If you try to draw a triangle with all obtuse angles, it won't be a triangle. We learned that the angles of a triangle have to add up to 180°. If you have more than one obtuse angle then two angles will add up to more than 180°. It could never be a triangle because the two sides that have to meet to close it are pointing away from each other.*
   Like this ╲__╱

4. A quadrilateral is like an equilateral triangle.
   I agree ✓   I disagree ✓   because: *We decided to agree because they are both polygons and the words sound alike. But we decided to disagree because they are different shapes. A quadrilateral has four sides, but an equilateral triangle has three sides that are the same length.*

5. All quadrilaterals are rectangles.
   I agree __   I disagree ✓   because: *Some quadrilaterals are trapezoids, parallelograms, rhombuses, or squares. They all have four sides. All rectangles are quadrilaterals.*

CUBING

Another strategy that encourages critical thinking and analysis is cubing (Neeld, 1986). The process of cubing allows students to examine a problem from six viewpoints. As Figure 9 (p. 112) shows, the viewpoints used in this strategy can be modified to meet various situations. Each viewpoint or prompt is written on one face of a cube Although the prompts can be modified to meet the objectives of many learning situations, the generic steps for the cubing strategy are listed next:

1. Select a topic to be introduced or reviewed
2. Examine it form various sides or viewpoints
   - *Describe* it (the process, event, features, traits)
   - *Compare* it (similar to or different from?)
   - *Associate* it (analogies, makes me think of?)
   - *Analyze* it (composed of? steps, procedures?)
   - *Apply* it (how can it be applied to other situations?)
   - *Argue* for or against it (support your position)
3. Have students informally write their responses
4. Limit the amount of time spent on each prompt

Procedures
- Demonstrate with the entire class initially and then have students work in small groups to "cube" a topic.
- Each small group can take one side of the cube, brainstorm their responses while a group appointed "scribe" jots down their thinking on square pieces of posterboard.
- These squares can then be taped together to form a cube. The groups can turn the cube and share their thinking about each side of the problem, issue, or event with the entire class. Turning the cube allows the students to react to various perspectives of the problem situation.
- Should a teacher prefer that each small group of students write about all six sides of the topic (as described in the next lesson), then each group member can take turns writing the group's responses and together the group members can construct their cube.
- Another variation is to provide already constructed cubes similar to the one shown in Figure 9 (p. 112) and provide students with Post-It notes to jot down their reactions. These notes can then be attached to the corresponding sides.

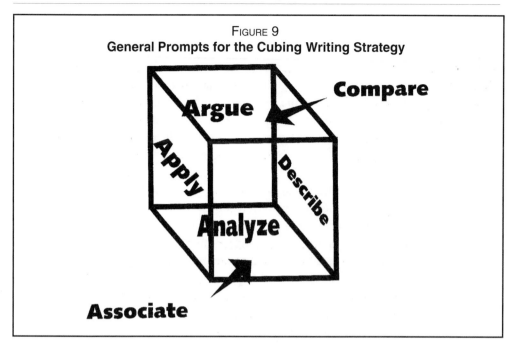

FIGURE 9
General Prompts for the Cubing Writing Strategy

A Sample Cubing Lesson in Science and Mathematics

One approach, modified to facilitate reflection during problem solving, is to have students respond to prompts in a sequential order. Cubing provides a structure for the students to consider various aspects of the investigation and how it relates to various mathematical and scientific concepts (Pugalee, DiBiase, & Wood, 1999). In one investigation, students are asked to explore the process of diffusion using observation, data tables, and graphing skills.

- Students will need three petri dishes, a potassium permanganate crystal, compass, and centimeter graph paper.
- Working in small groups, students are to draw three concentric circles one centimeter apart on the graph paper.
- In individual petri dishes place hot water, ice water, and water at room temperature.
- Carefully place the crystal in each dish and center the concentric circles on the graph paper at the center of each petri dish.
- Prior to placing the crystal in the solution, each group could do a "quickwrite" outlining their predictions. Have the students record the approximate radius of the cloud of the dissolved crystal for 30 minutes at two-minute intervals.
- Once the data have been collected, a cubing activity can be used to facilitate the discussion of the results. (See the same cubing question prompts below.)
- Heterogeneous groups of five or six students brainstorm and write down their responses to the prompts. Since there are six sides with questions or viewpoints, each student has the opportunity to serve as scribe.

- The sides are taped together to form a cube and then each group is called on to discuss its thinking. The following prompts might be used to lead students in discovering the properties of diffusion:
    1. *Organize* and represent the data you collected.
    2. *Describe* the differences you noticed in the results.
    3. *Analyze* the reasons for these differences.
    4. *Predict* what might happen if the petri dishes were allowed to sit until tomorrow.
    5. *Summarize* your observations based on the data you have collected and organized.
    6. *Explore* the topic by telling other types of investigations or observations that could be conducted.
- Responding to the questions in this order helps students organize the data that they have collected and begin exploring relationships and inferences. The prompts can be changed to fit a particular problem or situation. Having students write a brief synopsis of their findings and inferences promotes critical reflection.

References

Duffelmeyer, F. A. (1994). Effective anticipation guide statements for learning from expository prose. *Journal of Reading, 37* (6), 452-457.

Duffelmeyer, F. A., & Baum, D. D. (1992). The extended anticipation guide revisited (open to suggestion). *Journal of Reading, 3.5* (8), 654-656.

Goodman, J. (1992). Towards a discourse of imagery: Critical curriculum theorizing. *The Educational Forum, 56,* 269-289.

National Council of Teachers of English. (1996). *Standards for the English/language arts.* Urbana, IL: Author.

National Council of Teachers of Mathematics. (1998). *Principles and standards for school mathematics: Discussion draft.* Reston, VA: Author.

National Research Council. (1996). *National science education standards.* Washington, DC: Author.

Neeld (1986). *Writing.* Glenview, IL: Scott Foresman.

Pugalee, D. K., DiBiase, W. J., & Wood, K. D. (1999). Writing and the development of problem solving in mathematics and science. *Middle School Journal, 30* (5), 48-52.

Readence, J. B., Bean, T. W., & Baldwin, R. S. (1998). *Content area literacy: An integrated approach.* Dubuque, IA: Kendall/Hunt Publishing Co.

Weaver, D., & Alvermann, D. (2000). Critical thinking and discussion. In K. D. Wood & T. S. Dickinson (Eds.), *Promoting literacy in grades 4-9: A handbook for teachers and administrators* (pp.344-351). Boston: Allyn & Bacon.

Wood, K. D. (1992). Fostering collaborative reading and writing experiences in mathematics. *Journal of Reading, 36* (2), 96-103.

CHAPTER

13

Helping Struggling Readers and Writers

Research/Theory/Rationale. Far too many students in this country are working below grade level, and this number continues to rise (U. S. Department of Education, 2000). At the middle and high school levels, many of these readers and writers struggle through each class period experiencing little success with academic tasks assigned by teachers in the content areas. Although some are on the verge of failing, they can be provided with instructional experiences that enable them to experience some measure of success. These students need materials and assignments that are appropriate for their ability level and enough time during the day to practice reading and writing (Rhodes & Dudley-Marling, 1996; Routman, 1996). Moreover, research documents the reciprocal relationship between reading and writing and the importance of these two processes being taught and learned together (Tierney & Shanahan, 1991). Research has also shown that the more quality time students spend in meaningful literacy activities, the higher the achievement (Wood & Algozzine, 1994; Walp & Walmsley, 1995). The five teaching approaches suggested in this chapter can provide struggling middle and high school learners with opportunities to experience success with reading and writing.

PARTNER FLUENCY STRATEGY

If the reading ability of struggling readers is to improve, they must have ample time to practice fluency. Fluency refers to the smoothness of reading, the ability to read material with few interruptions due to inadequate word attack or word recognition problems. It is impossible to improve fluency if the material being read is too difficult for the student. Therefore, instructional materials must be available that are appropriate for students reading below grade level. Then, time needs to be allotted for students to use that material to practice fluent reading. The Partner Fluency Strategy created by Koskinen and Blum (1986) and modified for older readers by Wood (1998), is designed to help students develop reading fluency.

Procedures
- Pre-assign the struggling readers to pairs (or a group of three if the number is uneven) making certain that the students are sufficiently similar in ability to mutually benefit from instruction.

- Tell students that the purpose of this assignment is to help them become better readers and that improving the ability to read, as with any sport or activity, requires that they practice each day.
- Provide the students with passages that they can read with a minimal amount of assistance. These passages should be relatively short (50 to 100 words) so as not to be overwhelming to the students.
- Direct students to read their passages silently and then decide who will practice reading first. Students alternate the roles of reader and listener throughout the practice.
- When asked to serve as reader, the student reads the passage aloud to the partner three different times. The partner can assist with pronunciation and meaning if needed. Then the reader engages in self-evaluation answering the question, "How well did you read?" When asked to serve as listener, the student listens to the partner reading and then notes how the reading improved on the evaluation form shown in Figure 1 (p. 116). The only opportunity given for the partners to evaluate one another requires a positive response, not a negative one.
- After the third reading, instruct the students to switch roles and follow step three again.
- Circulate amongst the dyads to provide assistance and model effective fluent reading where appropriate.

Partner Comprehension/Retelling

While fluency is an important part of effective reading, it is insignificant if students fail to comprehend the passages to be read. One means for increasing students' understanding is to have students engage in retelling what they have read. The act of mentally or vocally rehearsing the content of a selection is a proven means of increasing students' recall and comprehension (Stahl, King, & Henk, 1991). The retelling form shown in Figure 2 (p. 117) is adapted from Koskinen, Gambrell, Kapinus, and Heathington (1988) and was originally designed for use with the fluency assessment form described in Figure 1. The form is useful when students engage in retelling any material and is appropriate for students of all ability levels.

Procedures
- Model the procedures for the whole class before implementation.
- Direct partners to whisper read together, to one another, or read a selection silently. For less able readers, the selections should be short and easy to manage – approximately 50 to 100 words.
- Instruct students to tell each other what they recall about the selection read. With narrative material, the focus is typically on the characters, setting, and events of the story. With expository material, the focus is frequently on the recall of the main ideas and details.
- Encourage partners to add to and embellish each other's retellings with analogies, anecdotes, and questions about the topic.

- Have partners work together to write their brief retelling in the space provided on the form. More than one whole class demonstration and modeling session may be needed for students to understand how to summarize information.

FIGURE 1
Partner Reading Assessment

Name_____ Partner _____

Date _____ We read _____

Reading #1
How well did you read? **Score!!**   **Good!**   **OK**   **Try Again**

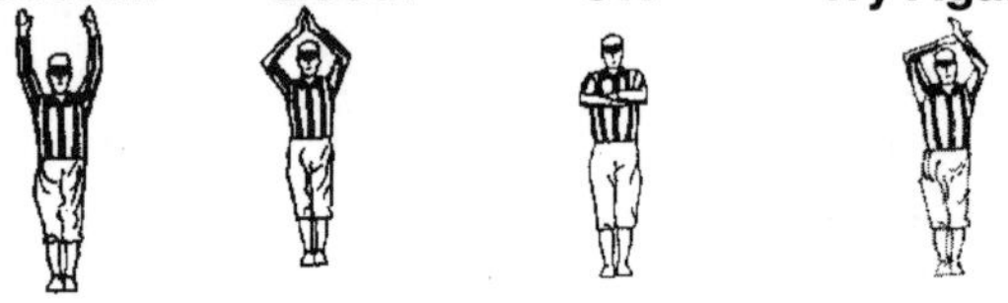

Reading #2
How well did you read

Reading #3
How well did you read?

How did your partner's reading improve?

Read more smoothly   _____

Knew more words   _____

Read with more expression   _____

Tell your partner one thing that was better about his or her reading.

_____

_____

_____

FIGURE 2
Retelling Form

Name _____   Date _____

I listened to _____

Choose one or more things your partner did well:

Fiction

_____ He or she told about the characters.

_____ He or she told about the setting.

_____ He or she told about events in the story.

_____ His or her story had a beginning.

_____ His or her story had an ending.

Non-fiction

_____ He or she told about the main ideas.

_____ He or she told about the details.

With the aid of your partner, retell the selection in your own words in the space below.

Reprinted with permission from Karen D. Wood and Allyn & Bacon Publishing Company.

Wordless Picture Books

Wordless picture books are one means of providing writing experiences for middle and high school students. Because they are a printless medium in book form, they are less intimidating to students who struggle daily to make sense of the printed word. Although traditionally thought of as appropriate only for elementary students, many wordless picture books have appeal for students in the upper levels. Procedures for using wordless picture books in the classroom as well as suggested book titles follow (Wood & Shea-Bischoff, 1997).

Procedures

- Introduce students to the world of wordless picture books by showing the work of various authors. Tell them that the reason these books do not have words is to enable the "readers" to invent their own story lines.
- Walk them through a book and ask them to orally tell what they think is going on in the pictures. You may need to "think aloud" your own version of the first few pages to model this new experience for them. For this modeling portion, it may be helpful to put the book on overhead transparences if it is being used with a large group of students.
- Then, beginning with the first page, ask students to tell you in sentence form what they think should be written on that page. Write their sentences underneath the picture on the transparency. Encourage the use of dialogue when appropriate and tell the students to "think like an author" since they are, in essence, writing their own book.
- After completing the last page, return to the beginning and ask the students to read the book in its completed form. This may be done chorally, in pairs, or individually depending upon the needs of the students.
- This book can be duplicated for each group member and used repeatedly to foster fluency and to provide additional practice with high frequency words.
- Other options include using post-it notes or index cards taped at the bottom of each page of the actual book to allow students working individually or in pairs to write, change, and modify their written versions. For ESL students and other students who are struggling with both our written and spoken language, it is beneficial to use smaller Post-It notes to label the concrete referent in the picture. Figure 3 (p. 119) is an excerpt of a student response to the wordless picture book *Tuesday* (Weisner, 1991). Figure 4 lists wordless picture books that are of interest to students in the upper levels.

FIGURE 3
**Excerpt from Responses to the
Wordless Picture Book** *Tuesday* **(Wiesner, 1991)**

1. It is quiet in the swamp and the turtle hears a noise.

2. Leapfrogs are flying over the pool.

3. They are flying through the sky every way.

4. The leapfrogs fly to a city.

5. A man hears the frogs flying outside his window.

FIGURE 4
Suggested Wordless Picture Books for Middle and High School Students

Anno, M. (1977). *Anno's journey.* New York: Collins.
Anno, M. (1978). *Anno's Italy.* New York: Collins.
Anno, M. (1982). *Anno's Britain.* New York: Philomel.
Anno, M. (1983). *Anno's USA.* New York: Philomel.
DePaola, T. (1979). *Flicks.* New York: Harcourt Brace Jovanovich.
Dupasquier, P. (1988). *The great escape.* Boston: Houghton Mifflin.
Goodall, J. S. (1975). *Creepy castle.* New York: Atheneum.
Goodall, J. S. (1976). *An Edwardian summer.* New York: Atheneum.
Goodall, J. S. (1979). *The story of an English village.* New York: Atheneum.
Goodall, J. S. (1979). *An Edwardian holiday.* New York: Atheneum.
Goodall, J. S. (1980). *An Edwardian season.* New York: Atheneum.
Goodall, J. S. (1983). *Above and below stairs.* New York: Atheneum.
Goodall, J. S. (1987). *The story of a high street.* New York: Atheneum.
Gross, M. (1971). *He done her wrong.* New York: Dover Publications.
Hoban, T. (1974). *Circles, triangles and squares.* New York: Macmillan/McGraw-Hill.
Hoban, T. (1983). *I read signs.* New York: Macmillan/McGraw-Hill.
Hutchins, P. (1971). *Changes, changes.* New York: Macmillan/McGraw-Hill.
Krahn, F. (1970). *Hildegard and Maximilian.* New York: Delacorte Press.
Krahn, F. (1977). *The mystery of the giant footprints.* New York: Dutton.
Krahn, F. (1978). *The great ape.* New York: Penguin.
McCully, E. A. (1987). *School.* New York: Harper & Row.
Monro. R. (1987). *The inside-outside book of Washington, D.C.* New York: Dutton.
Rohmann, E. (1994). *Time flies.* New York: Crown.
Spier, P. (1982). *Peter Spier's rain.* New York: Doubleday.
*Van Allsburg, C. (1984). *The mysteries of Harris Burdick.* Boston: Houghton Mifflin.
Wetherbee, H. (1978). *The wonder ring.* New York: Doubleday.
Wiesner, D. (1988). *Freefall.* New York: Lothrop, Lee & Shepard Books.
Wiesner, D. (1991). *Tuesday.* New York: Clarion Books.

* Contains some words.

Language Experience Caption Books

The language experience approach uses the students' own language as a basis for their reading materials (Allen, 1976). One way to implement this approach with struggling learners is through the use of caption books. Caption books are authored solely by the students themselves on a self-selected topic or a teacher-selected topic.

Procedures
- Decide upon a topic that correlates with the subject under study. For example, if the science class is studying pollution, the caption book assignment for the struggling learners should be on that topic.
- Instruct the students to draw or locate pictures that coordinate with the topic.
- Direct the students to use their own language and prior experiences as well as information learned from class discussions and demonstrations to write about each picture. In some instances, students may need peer assistance to write down their thinking. It is suggested that a student who is somewhat more capable than the struggling student be selected so that both students benefit from the experience and neither is intimidated nor bored by the strategy.
- Encourage students to use a repetitive pattern for each caption. For example, each line of the book could begin with "This is a picture of a . . ." or "Today in class, we learned that . . ." These patterns benefit those students who need practice with high frequency words that have no concrete referents, such as "were," "with," or "have."
- Allow students to use their newly created books as their reading material, taking turns reading them to their partners, reading them independently, and expanding the existing sentences with additional descriptive words and ideas.

Figure 5 (p. 121) is an excerpt from a language experience caption book for health. In this class the student who was reading well below grade level was able to work with a student tutor to develop a caption book representing what was learned in health class. The tutor and tutee worked together using technology in the form of word processing and online clip art to produce their own caption book.

Double Entry Journal

Another means of helping students write frequently is the double entry journal (Cox, 1996). This type of journal consists of two parts: (a) on the left side students record interesting parts or facts from the text, field trip, video, demonstration, or lecture, and (b) on the right side they record their responses and reactions. In some cases, it may be beneficial to allow students to work together to assist one another and to brainstorm ideas.

Procedures

- Introduce the concepts by modeling and thinking aloud the processes involved. Called shared writing (Routman, 1996), this allows the teacher and students to compose collaboratively but with the teacher serving as recorder, thinking and responding with the students. This step is best accomplished with an overhead projector for the class to observe and contribute.
- Tell the students to divide their paper in about one third of the space devoted to the left margin and two thirds for the remaining right side. On the left side, they will write down information from the textbook or other material (this could be information viewed or listened to as well). Struggling readers may be encouraged to get their information from pictures in the text in addition to other sources (viewed and heard) to offset the demands of the textbook reading.
- In the right column, instruct the students to write their reactions. These responses can include questions they have, experiences, surprise reactions, disagreements, creative thoughts, consequences, or applications to other contexts. Struggling writers can be encouraged to chart out their understanding by using pictures with labels or captions. During this portion of the lesson, the teachers may allow students to pair up, share what they remember, and discuss various ways of responding to the text.

Figure 6 (p. 122) is an example of a double entry journal in science in which a student tutor assisted another student who was struggling with the content.

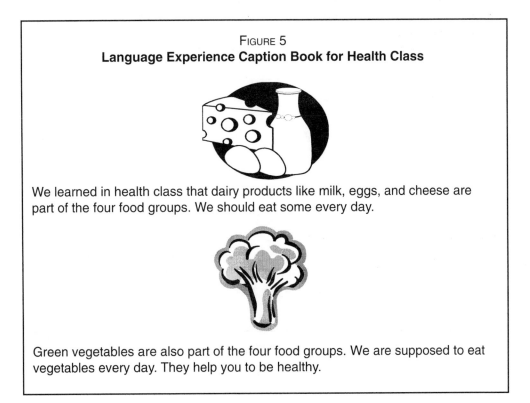

FIGURE 5
Language Experience Caption Book for Health Class

We learned in health class that dairy products like milk, eggs, and cheese are part of the four food groups. We should eat some every day.

Green vegetables are also part of the four food groups. We are supposed to eat vegetables every day. They help you to be healthy.

Figure 6
Double Entry Journal for Science

Notes (What the author said)	*Notes on Notes (What you say)*
Author's Main Points *"Biological Diversity" refers to the variety of life forms on earth threatened by many factors.*	**Questions You Want to Ask** *What are microorganisms?*
	Arguments (Statements that start with "but" or "however") *In the last paragraph it says, "However, since we only have one biosphere in which to live, what affects it eventually affects us all."*
Important Details *Animals, plants, insects, and microorganisms, as many as 100 million different species may exist.*	
Destruction of rainforests is major threat to biological diversity.	**Suggestions** (Ideas the author should have discussed, but didn't) *What are some examples of different species besides animals?*
Quotable Quotes *"Examples can be found from almost every area of the globe showing how populations, or even entire species, are at great risk."*	*Other knowledge, experience you have on the subject*
"Although rainforests cover less than 7 percent of the land surface of the earth, they are estimated to contain more than 50 percent of all species on earth."	*I know that manatees are also an endangered species.* *The Ozone Layer is also threatened.*
Author's Conclusions *The problems that affect the biosphere affect all of us.*	*Recycling is important to help save the earth.*
Details *World weather is changed by deforestation.*	**Evaluation** (Reasons you agree or disagree with the author) *I agree that people shouldn't destroy the rain forests because they are important to animals and humans.*
Rain forest species have potential for providing new medicines.	**Consequences** (Results or effects of the author's ideas) *I will tell my friends and neighbors to recycle.*
Carbon dioxide in the air leads to global warming.	

Reprinted with permission of Karen D. Wood and Allyn & Bacon Publishing Company.

Figure 7 (Wood & Shea-Bischoff, 1997) shows how two students, although functioning below grade level, worked together to synthesize information gleaned from several sources, a trade-book, the class textbook, a field trip, and a movie.

FIGURE 7

Partners: Kristin and Susan

The Facts	Our Response
11/18 Field Trip {At the exhibit, on special effects, we had our picture taken in a great big mug like we we were little-as huge cock-roach was in the backgrund. We tried on masks from Star Wars.	
11/20 Video {The video said even Speelburg beleved the alienin the film were real.	
11/23 Book {In our story, it said the government hid this from everyone.	

Human- Do you have TV's?
Zipp- Yes you earthlings. They are shaped as eyes.
Human- What do you do on your free time where you live?
Zipp- We hang out in arc cars and drive arond and go to the playground where we play bumper cars.
Human- Is there peace in your world?
Zipp- Yes there is peace in our world.

Excerpt from a Double Entry Journal with Varied Sources

References

Allen, R. V. (1976). *Language experience in communication.* Boston: Houghton Mifflin.

Cox, C. (1996). *Teaching language arts: A student and response centered classroom.* Boston: Allyn and Bacon.

Koskinen, P. S., & Blum, I. H. (1986). Paired repeated reading: A classroom strategy for developing fluent reading. *The Reading Teacher, 40* (1), 70-75.

Koskinen, P. S., Gambrell, L., Kapinus, B., & Heathington, B. (1988). Retelling: A strategy for enhancing students' reading comprehension. T*he Reading Teacher, 41* (9), 892-896.

Rhodes, L. K., & Dudley-Marling, C. (1996). *Readers and writers with a difference* (2nd ed.). Portsmouth, NH: Heinemann.

Routman, R. (1996). *Literacy at the crossroads: Critical talk about reading, writing, and other teaching dilemmas.* Plymouth, NH: Heinemann.

Stahl, N. A., King, J., & Henk, W. A. (1991). Enhancing students' notetaking through training and evaluation. *Journal of Reading, 34,* 614-622.

Tierney, R. J., & Shanahan, T. J. (1991). Research on the reading-writing relationship: Interaction, transitions and outcome. *Handbook of Reading Research, 2,* 246-280.

U. S. Department of Education, National Center for Education Statistics. (2000). *The Condition of Education 2000,* NCES 2000-602. Washington, DC: U. S. Government Printing Office.

Walp, T. P., & Walmsley, S. (1995). Scoring well on tests or becoming genuinely literate: Rethinking remediation in a small rural school. In R. Allington & S. A. Walmsley (Eds.), *No quick fix: Rethinking literacy programs in America's elementary schools* (pp. 177-196). Newark, DE: International Reading Association..

Wiesner, D. (1991). *Tuesday.* New York: Clarion Books.

Wood, K. D. (1998). Helping struggling readers read. *Middle School Journal, 29* (5), 67-70.

Wood, K. D., & Algozzine, B. (Eds.) (1994). *Teaching reading to high risk learners: A unified perspective.* Boston: Allyn & Bacon.

Wood, K.D., & Shea-Bischoff, P. (1997). Helping struggling writers write. *Middle School Journal, 28* (4), 50-53.

CHAPTER

14

Promoting Lifelong Readers Across the Curriculum

Research/Theory/Rationale. Recently, the Commission on Adolescent Literacy of the International Reading Association published a position statement outlining the kinds of literacy programs and support that adolescents deserve (Moore, Bean, Birdyshaw, & Rycik, 1999). They identified several principles for supporting adolescent literacy growth, one of which calls for "teachers who are trained to understand the complexities of individual adolescent readers, respect their differences, and respond to their characteristics" (p. 8). To create effective instructional environments that support this principle, teachers must consider the social, emotional, cognitive, and affective needs of adolescents (Carnegie Council on Adolescent Development, 1989). While these students tend to read less frequently (Mullis, 1992) and claim to be given less time to read self-selected books (Donahue, Voelkl, Campbell, & Mazzeo, 1999), it is important to help them view reading as a pleasurable and satisfying experience, a mindset critical for successful reading (Farnan, 1996). Furthermore, Ivey (1999) contends that even struggling middle school readers like to read if the materials are interesting and readable to them. Although the promotion of reading for pleasure is typically viewed as the domain of the reading/language arts teacher, the responsibility can and should be shared across the curriculum by teachers of all subject areas. Incorporating literature with subject area instruction can be an enriching experience for teachers and students alike without the burden of an added responsibility. This chapter answers questions that teachers typically pose about using literature across the curriculum and also offers strategy suggestions for using literature.

QUESTIONS ABOUT USING LITERATURE ACROSS THE CURRICULUM

How can I encourage students to read for pleasure?
- Create an atmosphere conducive to reading by designating a special corner of the room as the "reading nook" with a rug, reading lamp, bean bags, and a plant. Enhance the corner with colorful posters, mobiles, book jackets, and examples of students' written or artistic work.
- Make a wide range of books in terms of interest and readability readily available to students. When books are accessible and attractively displayed, students will tend to read more frequently (Clary, 1991).
- Read aloud to students to capture the attention of all ability levels.

- Although not widely familiar to most classroom teachers, interest inventories are useful in finding important information about students. Figure 1 is an adaptation from Readence, Bean, and Baldwin (1998) and Brozo and Simpson (1999). Information from the inventory can aid teachers in making book recommendations to students and in forming interest groups for specific projects. Teachers can easily modify this inventory to fit their own curricular goals and objectives.

Figure 1
Interest Inventory
(Modified from Brozo and Simpson, 1999;
Readence, Bean and Baldwin, 1998)
PART I

Directions: I want to know more about you – who are you, what you like to do, your future goals. Please finish these sentences:

1. If you were to see me after school, I would be

   _____
   _____

2. If you were to see me on weekends, I would be

   _____
   _____

3. _____ is my favorite TV show because_____

   _____

4. The kind of music I like is _____
5. When I graduate from high school, I want to

   _____

6. If I could go anywhere in the world, I'd go to _____
   because _____
7. My favorite book is _____
8. The last book I read was _____
9. My favorite part of the newspaper is _____
10. My favorite school assignments involve: doing projects, writing reports, conducting experiments/surveys; working with others; working alone; other

   _____

PART II

Directions: Put a plus + beside anything you may be interested in reading.

Sports _____	Animals _____
Science Fiction _____	Fantasy _____
Folklore _____	Romance _____
Cars _____	Adventure _____
Humor _____	Mystery _____
War _____	Art _____
Supernatural _____	Foreign Lands _____
Science _____	History_____
Poetry _____	Family Life _____
Plays _____	Theatre, Plays _____
Mathematics _____	Human Drama _____
Health Sciences ____	Music _____
Other_____	

- Allow students to self-select their books. While many reading experiences may be teacher-assigned, allowing students to choose their selections can be very motivating. Some teachers may feel anxious about the self-selection process, yet as readers gain experience in reading for pleasure, they tend to select more appropriate materials (Nell, 1988).
- Make time for reading using such strategies as DEAR (Drop Everything and Read), SQUIRT (Sustained Quiet Reading Time), or USSR (Uninterrupted Sustained Silent Reading). Students, teachers, and other adults spend 15 minutes or more daily engaged in reading – all at the same specified time.

Where can I find appropriate literature?
- Consult with your school media specialist.
- For an extensive selection of books, refer to

  Booklinks: Connecting Books, Librarians and Classrooms.
  www.ala.org/Booklinks/

  Price, A., & Yaakov J. (Eds.). (1995). *Middle and junior high school catalog* (7th ed.). New York: H. W. Wilson.

  Calvert, S. J. (1997). *Best books for young adult readers.* New Providence, NJ: R. R. Bowker.

- For an annotated list of picture books for older students, consult Martinez, M. G., Roser, N. L., & Strecker, S. (2000). Using picture books with older students. In K. D. Wood and T. S. Dickinson (Eds.), *Promoting literacy in the twenty-first century: A handbook for teachers and administrators in grades 4-9* (pp. 250-262). Boston, MA: Allyn & Bacon.

- For a thematic listing of adolescent books, refer to:

  Combs, M. (1997). *Developing competent readers and writers in the middle grades.* Upper Saddle River, NJ: Merrill.

- Refer to Figure 2 (p. 128) for other published sources.

How can I relate the literature to my instruction?
- Using the sources listed previously, find books related to the content topic you want to teach. Figure 3 (p. 129) lists examples of literature related to various subject areas.
- To entice students and assist them with their choices, give brief book-talks to acquaint students with the choices that are available. The media specialist or even fellow students can recommend books.
- Refer to the list below for examples of books on specified topics. While none are listed here, poetry and plays are additional types of literature that can be included in a thematic unit.

FIGURE 2
Sources of Literature for Middle and High School Classrooms

ALAN Review. Assembly on Literature for Adolescents. National Council of Teachers of English (published 3 times a year)

Appraisal: Science books for young people. Children's Science Book Review Committee (published 3 times a year)

Beers, K., & Samuels B. G. (Eds.). (1998). *Into focus: Understanding and creating middle school readers.* Norwood, MA: Christopher-Gordon Publishers, Inc.

Donelson, K., & Nilsen, A. P. (2000). *Literature for today's young adults* (6th ed.). New York: Addison Wesley Longman.

Dreyer, S. (1987). *The bookfinder: A guide to children's literature about the needs and problems of youth aged 2-15.* Circle Pines, NM: American Guidance Service.

Richardson, J. S. (2000). *Read it aloud!: Using literature in the secondary content classroom.* Newark, DE: International Reading Association.

Young adults' choices. (1999). Newark, DE: International Reading Association.

How can I keep track of my students' reading?
- Keep a record of book selections and response choices by using a Reader Response Form (Wood, 1994; 2001). This form provides a means for teachers and students to keep track of students' self-selected reading as well as the varied ways they may choose to respond to a book. These different and interesting alternative formats are welcome substitutes to the traditional "book report." As shown in Figure 4 (p. 130), the Reader Response Form provides choices such as dialogue journals, art projects, dramatic activities, mock book videos, critiques, blurbs, book jackets, and mobiles to name a few. If students do not complete a book, direct them to provide a brief, critical analysis of their reasons on the form. Some procedural suggestions are provided next to aid in the classroom implementation of the Reader Response Form.
- After promoting the benefits of your classroom or school-wide independent reading program, introduce the form by passing out copies to students and/or displaying a copy on the overhead projector. Explain to the students that this form will help them organize their reading selections and receive credit for their efforts.
- Each day or week, show examples and model the many ways students can respond to their reading.
- Place the forms near the book displays or reading corner where they are easily accessible to the students.

FIGURE 3
Literature Selections from Various Subject Areas

History
  The American Revolution
    O'Dell, S. *Sarah Bishop*
    Forbes, E. *Johnny Tremain*
    Collier J., & Collier, C. *The Bloody Country*
    Collier J., & Collier, C. *My Brother Sam Is Dead*
    Campion, N. R. *Patrick Henry: Firebrand of the Revolution*
    Meltzer, M. *The American Revolutionaries: A History in Their Own Words*
    Davis, B. *Heroes of the American Revolution*

Language Arts
  Working together/Collaboration
    Voigt, C. *Dicey's Song*
    Philbrick, R. *Freak the Mighty*
    Brooks, B. *The Moves Make the Man*
    Frank, A. *The Diary of a Young Girl*
    George, J. C. *Julie of the Wolves*
    Lowry, L. *Number the Stars*
    Ballard, R. D. *Exploring the Titanic*

Health/Science/Language Arts
  Death/Dying
    Carter, A. R. *Shelia's Dying*
    Lowry, L. *A Summer to Die*
    O'Brien, R. *Z for Zachariah*
    Craven, C. M. *I Heard the Owl Call My Name*
    Bennett, J. *The Haunted One*

- One option is to have students select the way they want to respond to a self-selected book and use the form to record their responses. Another option is to assign a reading selection (from a basal anthology, for example) and allow students to choose the way they want to respond.
- Students may be asked to share their books and methods of responding in small groups.
- The completed forms may be included in students' portfolios and shared with parents.
- Use samples of previous student work or a teacher-designed form to model the response options.
- Use the Reader Response Form to keep track of and give credit for students' reading. We recommend that grading of such responses be kept to a minimum. Instead encourage peer sharing and assistance if deemed necessary.
- *Remember, the primary objective is to reward and encourage reading as much as possible*!

FIGURE 4
Reader Response Form

Name _____   Class _____   Date _____

Title of book
_____

Author
_____

I chose this book because
_____

Number of pages: _____

I read the entire book ___ Yes   ___ No

I read the book ___ at home ___ at school ___ both

Reaction to the book				
1	2	3	4	5
Disliked		Okay		Really Liked

Choose the way you want to respond to this book.

Attach your response to this form.

- ❑ Newspaper article, advertisement
- ❑ Timeline of major events
- ❑ Take a position on an issue in the book
- ❑ Book jacket, poster, blurb
- ❑ My favorite part(s) is/are…
- ❑ My favorite character(s) is/are…
- ❑ Write a letter to a friend about the book
- ❑ Design a book jacket
- ❑ Write a skit, play, song, poem
- ❑ Describe an experience from the perspective of a character or thing in the book

- ❑ Talk show interview with _____
- ❑ If I could change one thing about the book it would be…
- ❑ After reading this book, I learned…
- ❑ Book review
- ❑ Book conference with teacher
- ❑ Conduct a book-talk for the class or group
- ❑ This book reminded of…
- ❑ I was puzzled by…
- ❑ Write in my journal (free response)
- ❑ Make a collage or mobile
- ❑ Other _____

STRATEGIES FOR USING LITERATURE ACROSS THE CURRICULUM

TAB Book Club Approach (Talking About Books in the Content Areas)

Book clubs in the classroom are opportunities for small groups of students to read and engage in lively discussions about a particular book, thereby reinforcing and expanding their understanding, knowledge base, and their appreciation of a literature selection (see Wood, 2000, for more information on book clubs). While book clubs have typically been implemented with much success in reading, language arts, or English classes, the TAB Book Club Approach (Harmon & Wood, 2001) is a means of integrating reading across the subject areas.

Procedures

- Locate appropriate trade books that relate to a specific topic. This approach works before, during, and even after a unit of study. Refer to the sources listed previously to find possible trade books.
- Introduce the TAB Book Club concept to students by explaining that reading and responding to trade books on related topics will help reinforce their understanding of key concepts and help them have a broader knowledge base.
- Model the process of responding and talking about books with the entire class. Read aloud a few opening paragraphs from the trade book as the class follows along. Then "think aloud" as you respond to the reading. For example, one teacher who used *The Boys' War* (1990) "thought out loud" with statements such as, "I wonder how many days it took for the people in the Midwest to learn about Lincoln's call for volunteers after Fort Sumter fell" and "I need to find out more information about the issue of states' rights causing the Civil War." Direct the students to read the next few paragraphs and to share their thinking by discussing different interpretations.
- Assign students to small heterogeneous book clubs. Then assign each group a different chapter in the book.
- Direct student groups to engage in the following sequential tasks of the TAB Book Club:

  —As they read the trade book chapter, students first use the TAB Chart to gather facts (Figure 5, p. 132) contains the sample chart used with *The Boys' War.* The chart helps students focus on important information and organize what they find. Students later transfer this information to a full-sized chart paper for their class presentations.

  —Once the groups complete the rough drafts of their TAB charts, they individually respond in their journals to one of several prompts provided by the teacher (Figure 6, p. 133).

  —Group members then participate in a book club discussion using their journal responses. Students take turns sharing what they wrote and asking questions of other participants. Then they collaboratively discuss and write a group reaction statement for the chapter on the TAB chart. Students can select one of the following prompts to write their group reaction statement.

—After reading this chapter, we feel that…

—After reading this chapter, we believe that the author should have considered…

—Create your own prompt.

—Each group transfers its information to a full-sized chart paper to share with the class. A group is the expert on its chapter since the other groups have not read it. In this formal presentation all group members stand up and each one talks about a segment of the TAB chart.

FIGURE 5
Sample Talking About Books (TAB) Chart
The Boys' War by Jim Murphy
Chapter 6: Home Sweet Home

What the Author is Telling Us about Camp Life . . .	Our Reaction to the Union and Confederacy
Sleeping conditions	They had a tent and there were about 10 soldiers in there. The blankets were frozen and wet. You see they had to sleep straight and close. Sometimes they couldn't sleep, so they smoked and sang.
Free time activities	They would go to sleep, gamble, write letters home. They had a lottery. They would race lice in their tents.
Religion	Most of the priests walked around reading the Bible to the people.
Money	Gambling was a good idea to make good money. Also buying and selling dollars was very good business.
Fraternization between Union and Confederate soldiers	They would sing songs and talk and gamble at night. Then during the day they were trying to kill each other. They would speak the same language and had the same religious beliefs. They learned to respect their enemies.

Group Reaction Statement
What we cannot believe is that the North and the South would fight in the afternoon and at night they would be friends. Maybe they killed the person they had chatted with at night. They would even share their rations. It was funny the way they slept like sardines. It was almost like a puzzle.

FIGURE 6
Sample Prompts
Writing Prompts for Response Journals

- What did you find new or interesting in this chapter?

- What do you want to know more about?

- Were there any parts you found boring? What were they? Why were they boring?

- How did the information in the chapter make you feel?

- What did the information in the chapter make you think about?

- Were some sections of the chapter difficult to understand? What questions do you have about this section?

- What connections can you make with this information? (self, text, world)

Language Charts

Promoting positive values can also be accomplished through the use of language charts (Roser, Hoffman, Labbo, & Farest, 1992) or inquiry charts (Hoffman, 1992) as an effective extension of book clubs where different groups read different trade books. Students engage in higher level thinking processes, such as summarizing, analyzing, and comparing, as they create their own language charts. This activity also allows students to express their own personal responses to what is read. Figure 7 (p. 134) provides an excerpt of a language chart that was used in conjunction with book clubs (Wood, 2000). The following guidelines are recommendations for implementing language charts in the classroom (Wood, 2001).

Procedures

- After book club groups have finished reading their books, the whole class comes together to create a language chart.
- Discuss different topics to include at the top of the matrix. These topics need to relate to the readings and may include questions, statements, or facts.
- Write the titles of the book selections read by the groups in the left-hand column of the language chart.
- Direct each book club group to discuss the topics on the matrix in reference to its own book. Have each group fill in the class language chart with information.
- After the groups have completed their sections of the language chart, facilitate a whole class discussion by focusing on the patterns, themes, and relationships that may emerge from the language chart.

Figure 7
Excerpt from a Language Chart

Title/Author/ Type	Characters	Main Problem(s)/ Issue(s)/Event(s)	How did their relationship change?	What was learned?
The Cay/ Theodore Taylor/ (Adventure)	Phillip, 11 years old, is ship-wrecked with Timothy, a West Indian.	Phillip doesn't trust Timothy at first and isn't nice to him.	Timothy helps Phillip when he goes blind.	That we are all human beings and deserve respect.
Crash / Jerry Spinelli/ (Sports)	Crash Coogan, a 7th grade football star; Mike, his friend and a prankster; Webb, a nerd who is picked on.	(1) Crash's grandfather has a stroke. (2) Mike and Crash pick on Webb for being different.	Webb gives Crash a present to help cure his sick grandfather and Crash helps Webb win the race.	That people who are differ-ent can be great friends.
Shiloh/ Phyllis Reynolds Naylor	Marty Preston, an 11-year-old; Shiloh, a dog nobody wants; Judd, the dog's mean owner.	Marty finds a mistreated beagle pup and hides it in the woods, away from his par-ents.	Marty offers to work for Judd so that he may keep the dog; he also agrees to keep quiet about Judd's deer hunting.	That lying only leads to more problems, but it is important to help animals and people.

References

Brozo, W. G., & Simpson, M. L. (1999). *Readers, teachers and learners: Expanding literacy across the content areas* (3rd ed.). Upper Saddle River, NJ: Merrill.

Carnegie Council on Adolescent Development. (1989). *Turning points: Preparing American youth for the 21st century.* New York: The Carnegie Corporation.

Clary, L. (1991). Getting adolescents to read. *Journal of Reading, 34,* 340-345.

Donahue, P. L., Voelkl, K. E., Campbell, J. R., & Mazzeo, J. (1999). *NAEP 1998 reading report card for the nation and the states.* U. S. Department of Education, Office of Educational Research and Improvement.

Farnan, N. (1996). Connecting adolescents and reading: Goals at the middle level. *Journal of Adolescent and Adult Literacy, 39* (6), 436-445.

Harmon, J. M., & Wood, K. D. (2001). Talking about books in content area classrooms: The T.A.B. book club approach. *Middle School Journal, 32* (3), 51-56.

Hoffman, J. V. (1992). Critical reading/thinking across the curriculum: Using I-charts to support learning. *Language Arts, 69* (2), 121-27.

Ivey, G. (1999). Reflections on teaching struggling middle school readers. *Journal of Adolescent and Adult Literacy, 42*(5), 372-381.

Moore, D. W., Bean, T. W., Birdyshaw, D., & Rycik, J. A. (1999). *Adolescent literacy: A position statement for the Commission on Adolescent Literacy on the International Reading Association.* Newark, DE: International Reading Association.

Mullis, I. (1992). *NAEP facts: Trends in school and home contexts for learning.* U. S. Department of Education, Office of Educational Research and Improvement.

Murphy, J. (1990). *The boys' war.* Clarion Books.

Naylor, P. R. (1991). *Shiloh.* Atheneum.

Nell, V. (1988). *Lost in a book: The psychology of reading for pleasure.* New Haven, CT: Yale University Press.

Readence, J. E., Bean, T. W., & Baldwin, R. S. (1998). *Content area literacy: An integrated approach.* (6th ed.). Dubuque, IA: Kendall Hunt.

Roser, N. L., Hoffman, J.V., Labbo, L. D., & Farest, C. (1992). Language charts: A record of story time talk. *Language Arts, 69,* 44-52.

Wood, K. D. (1994). *Practical strategies for improving instruction.* Columbus, OH: National Middle School Association.

Wood, K. D. (2000). Asset building in the classroom: An instructional perspective. *Middle School Journal, 31* (3), 53-56.

Wood, K. D. (2001). *Literacy strategies across the subject areas.* Boston: Allyn & Bacon.

15

Helping Students Learn From Listening and Viewing

Research/Theory/Rationale. Listening has long been considered one of the communication processes together with speaking, reading, and writing. Literacy educators today, however, also include viewing and visually representing as important language skills for success in our society (Flood, Brice, Heath, & Lapp, 1997; Standards for the English Language Arts, 1996). While research is scant on classroom viewing, studies have shown that students spend at least fifty percent of their time at school listening (Hyslop & Tone, 1988; Wolvin & Coakley, 1988). It is the primary mode by which students get directions and information from teachers and from others. Listening, coupled with viewing, is also the principal means for learning from videos, field trips, and demonstrations. Because many students frequently listen in an ineffective manner (Jalongo, 1991), it is important to highlight listening strategies by incorporating them into ongoing classroom activities. This chapter describes three approaches that can help students become stronger listeners as they view films, develop research skills, and listen to peers read.

COLLABORATIVE LISTENING-VIEWING GUIDE

The Collaborative Listening-Viewing Guide (Wood, 1994, 2001) is designed to assist students in learning information from what they see or hear as teachers conduct experiments (i.e., in science classes), show demonstrations (i.e., procedures to be followed in solving a mathematics problem), provide information on field trips (i.e., to a local historical site), invite guest speakers to lecture (i.e., in health class), and show videos (i.e., to introduce a selection in language arts). The guide is a framework for taking notes from information observed and/or heard. It can be used by teachers as an organized format to follow in presenting content. Conversely, it can be used by students to receive, record, and process the new content with the aid of their peers. The five phases used in this approach are described next.

Phase 1: Preview/Review Information
- To preview what is to come, decide whether this step will be a student-directed activity, a teacher-directed activity, or a combination of both.
- As a student-directed activity, brainstorm what students know about a particular topic. For example, a teacher may say, "Before we see this video-tape on the Vietnam War, let's find out what you already know. I'll organize your responses on the board."

- As a teacher-directed activity, present key concepts and vocabulary to be encountered in the subsequent lesson. A lead-in statement for this activity might be, "Since our demonstration today will be on static electricity, there are a few terms you will hear that warrant explanation. I will explain the definitions and show how they will be used in the context of our demonstraton."
- Sometimes a related field trip, video, or demonstration will follow a particular unit, chapter, or topic as a means of solidifying and extending the lesson. To review what was already learned, the teacher directive might be, "We have been studying Greece. Tell me what you remember about Greek customs, old and new, before we meet our guest who is a native of Greece."
- During this previewing or reviewing of information, students record relevant information on the guide.

Phase 2: Record (individually)
- Ask students to jot down significant concepts, phrases, or events as they are listening or viewing.
- Approximately one third of the left-hand side of the form is reserved for a verbatim transcription of what is heard and seen. Instruct students to write down important points in this column, making sure they are brief and using abbreviations when possible.
- Tell students to record notes in sequential order to facilitate the group elaboration activity in the next phase.

Phase 3: Elaborate (small groups)
- Ask students to join together in previously established small groups to elaborate on their verbatim transcription.
- Direct students to "put their heads together" to recall details, extend their abbreviated notes, contribute related information, and reorganize the new content in a meaningful way.
- Implement this phase as soon after the initial listening/viewing lesson as possible to insure that the significant information can be recalled.

Phase 4: Synthesize (whole class)
- After the groups have met to elaborate on the initially recorded information, bring the class together to provide a broader view of the topic.
- Begin this phase by saying, "What are some significant things we have learned from today's observation?"
- Reorganize this information in another format, such as a semantic mapping.

Phase 5: Extend/Apply (pairs)
- Allow students to work in pairs to extend and apply the newly learned information.
- Provide options for this phase, such as the following:
    1. compose a paragraph or two consolidating some of the information
    2. design a project related to the topic

3. develop a semantic map of the key concepts
4. write a play or skit
5. conduct further research on an aspect of interest to you and your partner

A Sample Guide

This accompanying guide in Figure 1 depicts an excerpt from a student/small group notetaking session during and after viewing a video on *Oceans* (Wood, 1994; Wood, Lapp, & Flood, 1992). In this instance, the video was used to provide background information for a science unit on the same topic.

FIGURE 1
Excerpt from a Guide for a Videotape

Class: *Science*
Student's Name: *Kevin*

Topic: *Oceans*
Other Group Members: *Lauren, Eric*

Preview/Review: *The world is really one big ocean. 70 percent is water—not as calm as it looks—always moving. Plants and animals (some weigh tons and some can't be seen) — can change salt water to fresh water. Ocean bottom is six miles below surface (from our school to fairgrounds). Atlantic, Pacific, Indian, Arctic, Antarctic are the names of the oceans.*

Record (Individually)	Elaborate (Small Groups)
World oceans Pacific is largest	Pacific, Atlantic, and Indian in order of size make up world oceans—also Arctic and Antarctic
Ocean scientists	Oceanographers are scientists who study the sea
Swimming easier	Swimming is easier because salt helps us float—contains common table salt
Blue whales	Ocean is home of largest animals that ever lived. Blue whales can be 95 feet. Smallest is only 1/25000 of an inch.
Three types of life: Nekton, plankton, and benthos (jellyfish; small drifting)	Nekton—can swim around like fish, squid, whales, seals. Barracuda can swim at 30 mph. Many fish can't live everywhere in ocean because of temperature and food supply.
	Plankton—floating, drifting plants and animals (jellyfish).
	Benthos—plants and animals that live on the bottom of the ocean—sponges, starfish, coral, and oysters—fixed to bottom and can't move.

(continued)

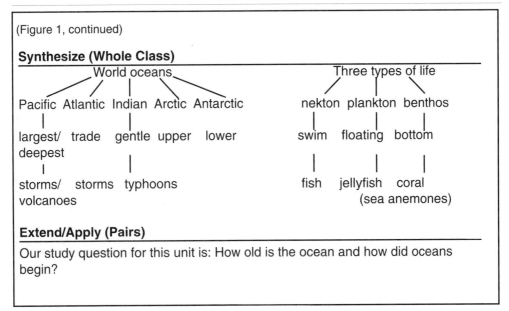

(Figure 1, continued)

Synthesize (Whole Class)

Extend/Apply (Pairs)

Our study question for this unit is: How old is the ocean and how did oceans begin?

INITIATING NOTETAKING FOR RESEARCH

This teaching strategy uses listening to help students learn how to take notes. It is the initial step in a process designed by Donna Maxim (1990) to guide students toward effective research practices. It teaches students how to take notes without copying by listening to information being read rather than reading it themselves.

Procedures

- Select a passage to read to the class. Selections may be found in magazines, such as *Time, U.S. News and World Report,* and *National Geographic,* or books. The books may be fiction or nonfiction as long as the excerpts contain enough information to make notetaking easy.
- Instruct the students to listen carefully while you read and to think about what is important in the passage.
- After reading, model how to take notes with the whole class. Think aloud what information you recall and write this down on chart paper. Then think aloud questions and reflections that the information elicits and write these down on the chart paper too.
- Read another selection from the book and have students take notes and generate questions.
- Continue this procedure until the passage is completed.
- Have students share their notes and questions with the whole class.
- Lead a discussion in which students consider what research projects they could do based on their notes and questions.

RADIO READING

Radio Reading is a strategy that promotes listening comprehension, oral reading practice, and summarization (Greene, 1979). Tierney and Readence (2000) recommend that Radio Reading be used in either a one-to-one or a group setting in language arts classes as well as content area classes. The following procedures represent an adaptation of Radio Reading that places a stronger emphasis on listening comprehension.

Procedures

- Select materials for Radio Reading that are instructionally appropriate for the class, but not too difficult.
- Tell students that in Radio Reading one student will read and everyone else will listen. Explain the responsibility of the reader by using a comparison of how radio announcers communicate to their audience. Tell the audience (the rest of the group) that they will not have a copy of the text and must therefore listen carefully.
- Help the radio announcer practice the selection he/she will be reading aloud to the group. Urge the student to practice reading aloud at home.
- Once the student is prepared to read, conduct the Radio Reading session.
- Encourage the audience to listen carefully as the reader reads the passage.
- After the reading, direct the audience to jot down notes on what they remember and to generate questions about the topic.
- The audience may ask the reader to reread certain sections for clarification.
- Conduct a group discussion of what was read by asking students to retell or summarize the passage.

References

Flood, J., Brice-Heath, S., & Lapp, D. (1997). *Handbook of research on teaching literacy through the communicative and visual arts.* New York: Macmillan.

Greene, F. P. (1979). Radio reading. In C. Pennock (Ed.), *Reading comprehension at four linguistic levels* (pp. 104-107). Newark, DE: International Reading Association.

Hyslop N. B., & Tone, B. (1988). Listening: Are we teaching it, and if so, how? *ERIC Digest, 3,* Bloomington, IN: ERIC Clearinghouse on Reading and Communication Skills.

Jalongo, M. R. (1991). *Strategies for developing children's listening skills* (Phi Delta Kappa Fastback Series #314). Bloomington, IN: Phi Delta Kappa Educational Foundation.

Maxim, D. (1990). Beginning researchers. In. N. Atwell (Ed.), *Coming to know: Writing to learn in intermediate grades* (pp. 3-16). Portsmouth, NH: Heinemann.

Standards for the English language arts. (1996). Urbana, IL: National Council of Teachers of English and Newark, DE: International Reading Association.

Tierney, R. J., & Readence, J. E. (2000). *Reading strategies and practices: A compendium* (5th ed.). Boston, MA: Allyn & Bacon.

Wolvin, A., & Coakley, G. (1988). *Listening* (3rd ed.). Dubuque, IA: William C. Brown.

Wood, K. D. (1994). *Practical strategies for improving instruction.* Columbus, OH: National Middle School Association

Wood, K. D. (2001). *Literacy strategies across the subject areas*. Boston: Allyn & Bacon.

Wood, K. D., Lapp, D., & Flood, J. (1992). *Guiding readers through text: A review of study guides*. Newark, DE: International Reading Association.

CHAPTER

16

Fostering Self-Expression Through the Arts

Research/Theory/Rationale. The arts have been a vehicle for self-expression and a means to communicate across cultures throughout the ages. The visual and communicative arts enable us to create and problem solve, understand and analyze the ideas of others, and develop a deeper connection across all of humanity (Flood, Brice-Heath, & Lapp, 1998). According to the National Endowment for the Arts (1993), schools with strong arts education programs have shown increased academic achievement in social studies, math, and English as well as a decrease in absenteeism and dropout rates. Because the arts serve as a universal language for all cultures and abilities, it may be that students who struggle with print can find success in other forms of self-expression, such as drawing, painting, writing, drama, or music. This chapter offers practical strategies for engaging middle and secondary learners in three areas of self-expression: art, drama, and gesture (Wood, Finke, & Douville, 1999).

TALKING DRAWINGS

One strategy for incorporating art across the subject matter areas is Talking Drawings (McConnell, 1993). This strategy asks students to make a drawing of their knowledge of a topic before and after reading and then to talk over their creations with a partner.

Procedures
- **Introduce.** Explain the purpose of the strategy. Tell the students to make a drawing before they read to illustrate what they already know about the topic and then again after they read to depict what they have learned from the reading. Explain how this process will help them remember what they have read as well as how their knowledge has increased.
- **Draw (Before).** Direct students to illustrate their visual images by drawing a picture of what they know about the topic.
- **Share.** Ask students to share drawings with two other classmates to discuss differences and similarities.
- **Discuss.** Conduct a whole class discussion in which students talk about their drawings.
- **Organize.** As a whole class activity, organize the information on a sheet of chart paper or on a transparency for the overhead projector. Use a semantic

— 142 —

map, a concept cluster, or an outline to present this information.

- **Read, View, Experience.** Direct students to read the designated text selection, watch a video, observe a demonstration, or go on a field trip. Ask them to note any new information they learn.
- **Draw (After).** Tell students to make another drawing to include the new information they have learned or to reconfigure their original drawing with the new information. Figure 1 represents both a "before" and an "after reading" drawing.
- **Share and Compare.** As students share their drawings with other students, have them explain the changes they made and the reasons for the changes. Encourage them to look back in the selection to lend support for their decisions.
- **Organize.** As a whole class activity, organize the new information in some form on chart paper or the overhead projector. This might take the form of another semantic map or web, depicting what the students have now learned about the key concepts. For the lesson on photosynthesis, depicted in Figure 1, the map of the key concepts would be more beneficial presented in the form of a plant, illustrating the key parts and processes.

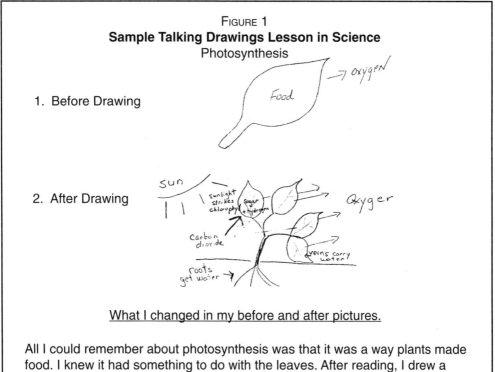

FIGURE 1
Sample Talking Drawings Lesson in Science
Photosynthesis

1. Before Drawing

2. After Drawing

What I changed in my before and after pictures.

All I could remember about photosynthesis was that it was a way plants made food. I knew it had something to do with the leaves. After reading, I drew a picture of a plant with the roots because that is how the plant gets water to the leaves. Then I showed how the leaf takes in carbon dioxide and gives off oxygen. I also showed how the sun is important in the whole process. It makes light energy divide into hydrogen and oxygen. The hydrogen and carbon dioxide combine and make simple sugar. Then, the oxygen is released in the air.

Reader's Theatre

Drama, another form of self-expression, provides students with an active means of learning content by using teamwork, critical inquiry, and imagination (Chilcoat, 1995; Doyle, 1993). Reader's Theatre is one form of dramatic expression whereby students create and read a script that depicts a conversation, a scene, or an action related to a story, a historical event, or some concept or event. The script contains different roles to be read, not memorized, by the students. It works well with all content areas to help students make connections to issues, historical figures, concepts, and events. Dialogues taking place between current individuals and historical figures (real or imaginary) also make interesting reader's theatre scripts to explore issues and concepts. For example, physicians debating health issues, physicists discussing laws, mathematicians arguing proofs in a reader's theatre format provide students with opportunities to develop thorough understanding of the concepts presented. In addition, introducing conflict into the dialogue helps students make connections as in a reader's theatre script of a conversation between Hitler, Lincoln, and Martin Luther King, Jr. (Wood, Finke, & Douville, 1999). Copeland (1991) provides the guidelines below for developing Reader's Theatre scripts.

Procedures
- **Select the source for the script.**
  - Historical and cultural events, scientific facts, mathematical discoveries, or literary descriptions can be used as the topic for a script.
  - Students research the topic by using textbooks, reference books, periodicals, journals, and the Internet.

- **Write the script.**
  - The teacher and the students can brainstorm what to include in the script.
  - Students can use a model script of a familiar story to write their own script.
  - The content should be interesting enough to keep the audience engaged or curious about what will happen next.
  - Students need to create scripts that contain more dialogue than action.
  - Students can use direct quotes from references and even their own expressions in their scripts.
  - The narrator in the script provides the setting, changes in scenes, or an explanation of actions.

- **Present the script to an audience.**
  - Before presenting the script to an audience, students must practice reading their parts with fluency, expression, and confidence.
  - Students can either sit or stand while presenting the script.
  - Body movements during the presentation are minimal. Students can step aside, sit down, or lower their heads to indicate that a character is exiting the scene.
  - Students may wear nametags to designate their characters.
  - Props and costumes are typically not used.

Figure 2 shows an excerpt from a reader's theatre script developed for social studies, specifically "The Early Explorers" depicting a conversation between King Fernando, Queen Isabella, and Columbus after he returned from his journey. To incorporate the use of technology, the majority of background information for the dialogue was derived from websites found on the Internet.

FIGURE 2
Excerpt from a Reader's Theatre Script for Social Studies:
The Early Explorers
Christopher Columbus Returns

Narrator: *With the support of Catholic monarchs, King Fernando and Queen Isabella had given Columbus ships to sail west into the Atlantic Ocean. Columbus promised that he would find a short way to reach the treasures of Asia. Columbus returned, bearing gifts for the king and queen.*
King Fernando: *Your demands for your voyage were quite lavish, but we understand you had a successful voyage.*
Columbus: *It was a great success, and as you promised, I expect to be knighted and made a viceroy of the lands I have found. Asia can be reached by sailing across the Atlantic and I have gifts for you from that land.*
Queen Isabella: *Your entry was quite amazing - horseback through the city! We have kept our part of the bargain. Now show us what you have found.*
Columbus: *I am certain you will be extremely pleased with the gifts I have for you. In fact, I have gold, spices, and the six Indians that I wrote to you about. These Indians are heathens and will need to be taught about God. They actually believe that I came down from heaven! When you see them, you will realize how valuable they are as strong, hard workers. But first, take a look at this gold.*

Reader's Theatre and Art

In addition to using text to recreate historical events, paintings may be used as stimulus for creating a script or dialogue about the event. For example, in Brumidi's 1878 painting, *Landing of Columbus,* displayed in the U.S. Capitol, Columbus is walking ashore. Individuals representing the different people groups depicted in the painting could become characters in a reader's theatre script. The script could be created to depict the many possible thoughts, feelings, and factual events that occurred.

Other paintings that might serve as a stimulus for reader's theatre scripts include

- *Defense of the Sacrament* expressing how the Spanish saw themselves a defenders of Catholicism
- *The Battle of Lexington* allows students to gain insight into the experience of emotions and issues of war, injury, and death
- *The Signing of the Declaration of Independence* provides students with an opportunity to take on the roles of the founding fathers and express the emotion, support, and hesitations related to this significant event
- *A Tough Story,* by John G. Brown, illustrates the hard life of immigrant children

- *Washington Crossing the Delaware* showing the conditions of this event gives students an opportunity to explore the struggles faced by these men

GESTURE AND PANTOMIME

Douville and Finke (2000) advocate the use of dramatic gesture, such as pantomiming, to help students to interpret information, solving problems, and physically and emotionally representing the roles of historical figures and events. Using prior knowledge and newly learned information, students can work together to represent abstract ideas in creative ways that reinforce and extend their understanding of a topic (Douville, 1998; Wolf, Edminston, & Encisco, 1997). Douville (1998) describes one variation of pantomime, called Procedural Pantomime, which is useful in different content areas. Students use body movements and other nonverbal actions to explain a process or procedure in science, events leading up to some historical moment, or steps involved in solving a mathematical problem. Wood, Finke, and Douville (1999) provide the example below of how Procedural Pantomime can work to explain the process of photosynthesis.

Example
- Four students perform the pantomime by taking on the roles of carbon dioxide, water, the sun, and a growing plant.
- The student representing carbon dioxide does so by making a hissing sound and mimicking the undulating movement of a gas.
- The "water" student can mimic falling raindrops.
- To represent the sun, the student can open his arms wide as if to embrace the elements of carbon dioxide and water.
- The last student, representing a growing plant, can arise slowly from the group.
- The pantomime can also be used to illustrate what happens when one element is missing. For example, as the "water" student moves away from the group, the "growing plant" student can collapse on the floor.
- The teacher can ask students from the audience to explain the process and to make suggestions to the actors.

References

Chilcoat, G. W. (1995). Using panorama theatre to teach middle school social studies. *Middle School Journal, 26* (4), 52-56.

Copeland, K. (1991). *Guidelines for incorporating reader's theatre.* Unpublished manuscript, University of Illinois at Urbana-Champaign.

Douville, P. (1998). *Bringing text to life: The effects of a multi-sensory imagery strategy of fifth-graders' prose processing and attitude reading.* A research report presented at the 43rd Annual Meeting of the International Reading Association, Orlando, FL.

Douville, P., & Finke, J. (2000). Literacy as performance: The power of creative drama in the classroom. In K. D. Wood & T. S. Dickinson (Eds.), *Promoting literacy in the twenty-first century: A handbook for teachers and administrators in grades 4-9.* (pp. 370-381). Boston: Allyn & Bacon.

Doyle, C. (1993). *Raising curtains on education.* Wesport, CT: Bergin and Garvey.

Flood, J., Brice-Heath, S., & Lapp, D. (1998). *Handbook of research on teaching literacy through the communicative and visual arts.* New York: Macmillan.

McConnell, S. (1993). Talking drawings: A strategy for assisting learners. *Journal of Reading, 36* (4), 260-269.

National Endowment for the Arts. (1993). *Arts in schools: Perspective from four nations.* Washington, DC: Author.

Wolf, S., Edminston, B., & Encisco, P. (1997). Drama worlds. Places of the heart, head, voice, and hand in dramatic interpretation. In. J. Flood, S. B. Heath, & D. Lapp (Eds.), *Research on teaching literacy through the communicative and visual arts* (pp. 492-505). New York: Simon & Schuster, Macmillan.

Wood, K. D., Finke, J., & Douville, P. (1999). Literacy as self-expression: Interpreting the subject areas through the arts. *Middle School Journal, 30* (4), 68-72.

17

Using Technology to Integrate Reading and Writing Across the Curriculum

Research/Theory/Rationale. In today's world it is essential that we train our students to become proficient in the technology used to access information (Reinking, Labbo, & McKenna, 1997). In this way, the basic ability to utilize computers and other technology can be mastered so students can use this ability to engage in literacy tasks. Computers can be used to enhance students' learning to enable them to achieve the two most important outcomes of using technology: communication and comprehension (Beach & Lundell, 1998; Wepner, Valmont, & Thurlow, 2000). Three methods for using technology to integrate reading and writing across the curriculum are described in this chapter (Nichols, Wood, & Rickelman, 2001).

The first strategy uses an anticipation guide (Readence, Bean, & Baldwin, 1998; Tierney, & Readence, 2000), a series of statements to which students respond both before and after reading, to prompt computer-based threaded discussions. The second strategy shows how collaborative learning can improve students' ability to seek out information from various sources in the writing of a composition or a research paper (Wood, 1998). The final portion of this chapter shows how a single classroom computer can be used to maximize participation from an entire class (Rickelman & Caplan, 2000).

THREADED DISCUSSIONS

One means of incorporating technology with writing and reading is through the use of threaded discussions. Threaded discussions, which are a form of computer-mediated communication (CMC), are designed to promote collaboration and interaction among students through printed discussions, as well as provide an environment for active engagement in literacy activities (Barron & Lyskawa, 1998; Beach & Lundell, 1998). While a content-related problem, task, or question can be used to prompt a threaded discussion in a classroom, an anticipation guide (also referred to as a reaction guide) is a viable means to stimulate students' critical thinking abilities before, during, and after the reading. Anticipation/reaction guides (described in detail in Chapter 12) are a series of five to eight statements that reflect the key concepts of a given unit of instruction. These teacher-developed guides are designed to activate students' existing knowledge and beliefs prior to reading and provide purpose by serving as a guide during reading (Readence, Bean, & Baldwin, 1998; Tierney, & Readence, 2000). Figure 1 (p. 149) illustrates the eight anticipation guide statements developed for the book *Hatchet* (Paulsen, 1987) and used as prompts for an online, threaded discussion between the students and each other and the teacher as well. Figure 2 is an excerpt from this threaded discussion.

FIGURE 1
Anticipation Guide Statements for Paulson's *Hatchet*
Used to Prompt Threaded Discussion

1. A 12-year-old has a lot to say to his/her mother before he leaves on a vacation.
2. Secrets destroy a family.
3. It is difficult to tell when someone has a heart attack.
4. A child has difficulty getting over a divorce.
5. Pilots let passengers fly a plane if they want to.
6. Young adolescents say and do things just to hurt their parents.
7. A flight to Canada for a summer vacation is a lot of fun.
8. A person can handle the most severe emergency situations.

FIGURE 2
Excerpt from a Threaded Discussion
Based on Anticipation Guide Statements

WELCOME
This is an online anticipation reaction guide to be used for Chapter 1 *Hatchet*. Students should post their response and reasoning for each statement. If someone posts a reaction different from yours, please respond. Please post any comments, reflections, or anticipated responses to the upcoming chapter. Once you have read the chapter, please respond again, based on the information provided in the text.

The content frame shows the titles of all articles posted to the discussion. Selecting a title will cause the corresponding article to be loaded into this frame.
You may also: Post a new article (starting a new thread)
                       Search the articles for a word or pattern
In addition, each article has links to let you reply to it (continue the thread) and navigate the article list.
Note: You may need to reload this page to see the most current entries.
[Home|Contents|Search|Post|Reply|Next|Previous|Up]

Please agree or disagree with the following statement and tell why.
From: Ms. Endres
Date: 11/13/00
Time: 1:15:07 PM
Remote Name: 152.15.145.95

(continued)

(Figure 2, continued)

Comments
A 12-year-old has a lot to say to his/her mother before he leaves on a vacation.

From: Rodnico
Date: 11/13/00
Time: 1:24:47 PM
Remote Name: 152.15.145.95

Comments
I disagree. I would not have much to say to my mom, because I would just be ready to go.

From: Sabrina
Date: 11/13/00
Time: 1:27:58 PM
Remote Name: 152.15.145.95

Comments
I agree with the statement and disagree with Rodnico. I always talk to my mom and I would have a lot to talk about before I went on vacation. We would talk about what we would do and what I would need to take. Rodnico wouldn't you be excited about the vacation?

From: Sabrina
Date: 11/14/00
Time: 3:07:22 PM
Remote Name: 152.15.145.95

Comments
The book disagrees with the statement and also disagrees with me. On page 7 of the text it states, "A drive in silence, a long drive in silence. Two and a half hours of sitting in the car, staring out the window..."

From: Ms. Endres
Date: 11/14/00
Time: 3:08:52 PM
Remote Name: 152.15.145.95

Comments
Why did Brian differ from you? You said that you always talked to your mom, why doesn't Brian have a lot to say?

From: Sabrina
Date: 11/14/00
Time: 3:10:15 PM
Remote Name: 152.15.145.95

Comments
Because, Brian blames his mom for the divorce. Something to do with a "Secret."

(continued)

(Figure 2, continued)

From: Kathy
Date: 11/13/00
Time: 1:29:10 PM
Remote Name: 152.15.145.95

Comments
I agree with the statement. I would have a lot to say before I left. I would talk about all of the things that we would do on the trip.

From: Rodnico
Date: 11/13/00
Time: 1:30:44 PM
Remote Name: 152.15.145.95

Comments
I see what Kathy and Sabrina are talking about, but I just don't usually talk to my mom a lot. I don't think I would have much to say.

Using Multiple Literacy Sources and Collaborative Learning to Write a Research Paper

The ability to locate, interpret, and synthesize information from a number of sources (e.g. the Internet, e-mail interviews, public television broadcasts, trade books, etc.) referred to as multiple source or information literacy (Breivik & Senn, 1994; Cohen, 1995), is essential to middle and high school students who are required to compose research papers in many subject areas. The use of collaborative learning in the form of flexible grouping methods can make the task of researching varied sources and composing a paper more palatable for the varied ability levels in a given classroom. The procedures to follow help students gain practice in seeking out and synthesizing information from multiple sources by using a "communal writing" (Wood, 1998) wherein students are assigned to heterogeneous groups of four or five to put their heads together in the composition of a single product. The teacher circulates among the groups and guides the writing. Subsequent practice sessions can proceed to pairs and then finally independent practice when the teacher feels the students have the necessary skills.

Learning About the Finished Product/Teacher Modeling (Whole Class)
- Begin by displaying at least one sample of a finished product via an overhead projector or a handout and walk the students through the organization and elements reflected in the composition. It is helpful to show examples of research reports that contain negative elements (e.g., one or two sources, copying from a source, lack of coherence, etc.) Many classes may need additional practice in how to take information and put it in their own words.

Teacher "think alouds" may be useful for this purpose, and a number of brief exchanges may be needed to ensure that students can engage in this form of self-recitation. Figure 3 is an example of a collaborative composition using multiple sources of information.

FIGURE 3
Sample Collaborative Research Composition Using Multiple Sources
Thomas Jefferson

Interesting Facts About His Childhood
Thomas Jefferson was born on April 13, 1743, in a place called Shadwell. Shadwell is located in Albemarle County, Virginia. His relatives immigrated to America from Wales. Thomas Jefferson had six sisters and one brother. (BOOK: *Thomas Jefferson: A Life*)
Thomas Jefferson went to many schools as a child. He learned how to read and write at Tuckahoe school and from teachings from his father. He also learned classical and modern languages when he was young. Thomas Jefferson still liked to do regular things that kids today do, like horseback riding, dancing, and playing the violin. He attended William and Mary College when he was 17. He married Martha Wayles Skelton. They had six children, but only two lived to become grown-ups. (WEBSITE: encarta.msn.com).

What Thomas Jefferson Did for America
While a member of the Continental Congress, Thomas Jefferson began to write a document to free slaves, even though no one else agreed with him. He stopped the trading of slaves also. In 1779, Thomas Jefferson was elected as the Governor of Virginia. (BOOK: *Thomas Jefferson: A Life*)
Thomas Jefferson was the third President of the United States. Some people say that he was the founder of the Democratic Party (MOVIE: *Thomas Jefferson*). He was very concerned with people's freedom, so he wrote about certain human rights. These rights are life, liberty, and the pursuit of happiness. Thomas Jefferson also wrote the Declaration of Independence. This gave America freedom from England, and is the reason for our holiday on the fourth of July (CD-ROM: *Encyclopedia Brittanica*).

Little Known Facts
Thomas Jefferson was the founder of the University of Virginia. He also is the founder of the United States' modern system of money and currency. (BOOK: *Thomas Jefferson: A Life*)

Compiled and Composed By

Santonio = Books	Elise = Videos
Laquisha = Internet	Demarcus = CD rom

References
Burns, K. (Producer). (1996). *Thomas Jefferson. Monticello*. Retrieved January 18, 2001 from the World Wide Web: http://encarta.msn.com/find/Concise.asp?z=1&pg=2&ti=0498c000
Randall, W. S. (1993). *Thomas Jefferson: A life*. New York: Holt.
Thomas Jefferson. Abstract from: Encyclopedia Brittanica 2001 Standard CD-ROM.

Learning About Resources (Whole Class)
- Before the actual writing of the paper, hold several sessions with the teacher and/or media specialist teaching, modeling, and demonstrating to the students how to seek out information from a variety of sources.

Assigning Students to the Research and Writing Groups (Small Group)
- Assign students to heterogeneous groups of four to six and allow them to physically group their desks together to undertake this assignment. Either give them the topic(s) under study or have the groups select a unit-related topic of their choice.
- Have the students in each group decide who will go to which source for the information. For example, a student proficient in Internet use might select that source. On the other hand, an avid reader might feel more comfortable looking at trade books. Students with limited English proficiency or other struggling learners may be paired with another group member to assist with the research process. Flexible grouping in this instance takes the form of "grouping within the group" to facilitate learning.
- Next, the groups get together to discuss their findings after sufficient time is provided either in class, in the media center, or at home to gather the preliminary information. Group members decide how to organize the information. Notice in Figure 2 how the students grouped information about Thomas Jefferson in three categories: *Interesting Facts About His Childhood, What Thomas Jefferson Did for America*, and *Little Known Facts*.
- Group members can then be asked to contribute what they found related to pre-selected sub-areas and decide how and where to put related information.
- Students can alternate the role of "recorder" or "typist" for each section of the report, carefully writing down related information and the source from which it came. In the example shown, information was entered into a word processor by a designated recorder.
- Then students can assume various roles such as "proofreader," "editor," or "final draft writer" to complete the finished product.

Assigning Students to Partner Writing Groups (Pairs)
- After at least one opportunity to research and write in small groups as described previously, the teacher may feel that the students are able to engage in this process with the aid of a partner. Generally, the partner will be similar in ability level, with the differences not too great to cause either intimidation or boredom. Ideally, both students should be able to help each other and benefit from the experience as well. Two students rather than a group of five or six will then undertake the subsequent, subject-related research assignment.

Releasing Responsibility to Each Student (Individual)

- The final phase of any direct instruction or gradual release of responsibility model is to allow students to apply the skill learned on their own in similar or other contexts, without the aid of peer or teacher assistance. With the multiple source research assignment, the goal is to create students who are "resource experts," sufficiently aware that many resources exist and how to synthesize them into a coherent composition. Before sending the students on their own, teachers should be sure they have provided sufficient scaffolding to ease students into the assignment.

PROMOTING CLASS-WIDE PARTICIPATION WITH A SINGLE COMPUTER

A problem many teachers face with using computers in their classroom is that the number of students who can work together on a single computer is limited. For instance, if a teacher has access to three computers in his/her classroom, three students can work independently, or six students can work in pairs. Usually there is not enough room in front of the monitor for more students to take part. Whole class demonstrations are limited, since only one student can "work" the computer, so classes often move to lab settings, where technology resource teachers take over the teaching.

Two strategies developed by teacher Bob Caplan, Georgia's Microsoft Teacher of the Year, and reported in Rickelman and Caplan (2000) make one computer serve a class.

Karaoke Poetry

Karaoke Poetry is a way to blend a unit on poetry appreciation with computer technology. The procedures are based on a progam called *New Kid on the Block* that uses the poetry of Jack Prelutsky. This program includes 17 poems over 8 hours of classroom instruction.

- Use one computer with Internet access attached to two 27" monitors set up on portable stands,
- Show the poems to be studied on the screen with *hotspots*, words that are clicked on to begin an animated sequence. (Generally two poems can be studied in a single class period)
- With the sound turned off, have the students engage in choral reading while the text is highlighted on the screen. (similar to a bouncing ball sing-along)
- Then the class examines each hotspot, discussing the part of speech, and why the author and programmers chose each. (For instance, nouns and verbs would be logical choices, since they often refer to concrete movements that would be simple to capture on the computer. Conjunctions, on the other hand, would be difficult to animate. So you would expect that most hotspots would be linked to concrete words.)
- Each student is actively engaged during class by assuming a number of different roles. For instance, a student could be assigned to be a guest

clicker, and he/she would move the mouse over the hotspot and click. A new clicker could be chosen for each page of text. Other students could be assigned the role of scribe, and they would keep track of how many hotspots are assigned to each part of speech.

- After a poem has been read several times, and the hotspots have been explored, students are assigned to write in their journals, discussing the poem, describing their favorite hotspots, and self-reflecting on the message contained in the poem.

Another software program originally intended for individual use that can be adapted for whole class involvement is Broderbund's *Where in the USA is Carmen Sandiego?* In this program students use geography cues to chase a criminal around the United States. Shown next are ways the program can be modified to enable a whole class to take part in reading, writing, and problem-solving tasks for an entire class period.

- Each student is assigned a job while viewing the program to promote active engagement.
- Ten students are assigned the *competitive scribe* role, bidding against each other to determine the suspect's next geographic move.
- Correct guesses yield points, which are tabulated by ten *point scribes*, one assigned to each competitive scribe to track their progress. The point scribes meet after the program ends to determine which competitive scribe had the most points.
- Five students are assigned the role of *detective scribe*, and their job is to gather evidence to secure a search warrant for the correct suspect.
- A fourth group of *research scribes* uses research materials supplied with the software to judge the correctness of the competitive scribes' guesses. Students exchange roles in subsequent classes for variety.

References

Barron, A., & Lyskawa, C. (1998). *Microsoft frontpage*. Cambridge, MA: International Thomson.

Beach, R., & Lundell, D. (1998). Early adolescents' use of computer-mediated communication in writing and reading. In D. Reinking, M. McKenna, L. D. Labbo, & R. D. Kieffer (Eds.), *Handbook of literacy and technology: Transformations in a post-typographic world* (pp. 93-114). Mahwah, NJ: Erlbaum.

Breivik, P. S., & Senn, J. A. (1994). *Information literacy: Educating children for the 21st century*. New York: Scholastic.

Cohen, P. (1995). Putting resource-based learning to work. *Education Update, 37*, 6.

Nichols, W. D., Wood, K. D., & Rickelman, R. J. (2001). Using technology to integrate reading and writing/Out of research-Into practice, *Middle School Journal, 32* (5), 45-50.

Paulsen, G. (1987) *Hatchet*. New York: Puffin Books.

Readence, J. E., Bean, T. W., & Baldwin, R. S. (1998). *Content area reading: An integrated approach* (6th ed.). Dubuque, IA: Kendall Hunt.

Reinking, D., Labbo, L., & McKenna, M. (1997). Navigating the changing landscape of literacy: Current theory and research in computer-based reading and writing. In J. Flood, S. Brice-Heath, & D. Lapp (Eds.), *Handbook of research on teaching literacy through the communicative and visual arts,* (pp. 77-92). New York: Simon & Schuster, Macmillan.

Rickelman, R. J., & Caplan, R. M. (2000). Technological literacy in the intermediate and middle grades. In K. D. Wood & T. S. Dickinson (Eds.), *Promoting literacy in grades 4-9: A handbook for teachers and administrators* (pp. 306-316). Boston: Allyn & Bacon.

Tierney, R. J., & Readence, J. E. (2000). *Reading strategies and practices* (5th ed.). Needham Heights, MA: Allyn & Bacon.

Wepner, S. B., Valmont, W. J., & Thurlow, R. (Eds). (2000). *Linking literacy and technology: A guide for K-8 classrooms*. Newark, DE: International Reading Association.

Wood, K. D. (1998). Flexible grouping and information literacy: A model of direct instruction. *North Carolina League of Middle Schools Journal, 19* (2), 2-5.

A Final Note

This collection of practical and functional instructional strategies should be a resource to which you will turn regularly. The activities can be readily implemented in all subject areas. We have grounded each of the chapters in a brief review of related research and theory, provided descriptions or step-by-step procedures of each strategy and then, where needed, given at least one sample lesson illustrating the applicability to varied disciplines. Had space permitted, many more sample lessons could have been provided showing the versatility of the strategies and the creativity of classroom teachers across the country.

Most of the strategies described can be adapted for any grade level and any discipline. They can be modified to coordinate with course objectives and time constraints. The variable determining their application rests with the goals of the teacher and the ability levels and needs of the students. Some strategies are more appropriate for students who are struggling with print; while others are more appropriate for students functioning on or above grade level. Common to all of the strategies is some form of reading and/or writing practice. We believe that classrooms at the middle and high school levels need to be reading and writing intensive; that is, some form of both reading and writing practice is essential every class period, every day, if students' literacy is to be improved.

The standards governing all areas of study uniformly advocate the integration of reading and writing across the curriculum. Literacy is the foundation for all subject areas, and it is through meaningful reading and writing activities that content becomes more comprehensible, engaging, and relevant. This book provides a repertoire of proven ways to integrate reading and writing that will help you be a more effective teacher and, most importantly, help your students be more effective learners.